Amber Alert

Judge Ordered Kidnapping

AleahRN

"A POWERFULLY COURAGEOUS BOOK,

Aleah's voice is so real; it is reality itself packed with meaning that we need to simply pay serious attention to. Her pain and the manner she expresses her story, described minute by minute, her direct, compact inner manner with which we hear her voice.

If this injustice has and is taking place, again and again, children are torn away from their parents, without any reason, legal or not, how does this stand in our society?
Her purpose is alive and kicking!

What Aleah and I have in common is that I a good father, had my then 7 year old daughter Leah, unjustly stolen from me in 2007 permanently by the same judge,
Esther Morgenstern and her same cartel that rigged my domestic violence and custody case in her domestic violence court."

Artemis Schwebel, Artist/Father

"When Brooklyn Judge Esther Morgenstern kidnapped my daughter out my life, it felt like she murdered her. When I found Aleah's book I nearly cried and I'm a big guy. I can bench press over 500 lbs. Aleah has helped me deal with my suffering, and my child being stolen out my life 10 years ago."

Kevin Topsey-Father

" A well written book and it proves that justice is not always right.
These are stories that the American public does not hear about, and
the media hides. This is a tragic story of a good mother being
destroyed by a judge's poor and bad judgments."
-T. Porter, NY

"I just had given this information of "family court crimes" to a
colleague who was doing a little evaluation and research on this; and
he in reality bought me breakfast because I discovered it for him. I
feel strongly about this and would love reading more. It's extremely
useful for me. Large thumb up for addressing this passed over topic"
- G. Fremont, NY

"Two Words, "Best Seller!" This is a MUST READ! It was an
incredible story and I am so touched and appreciative that you have
shared your story because it is truly one that needs to be heard! I
believe your story relates to mothers everywhere across the world
and that you will cross and reach nationwide levels with your story!

I admire your courageous fight and continued determination for
happiness and justice. Your fight for peace within yourself will
impact so many women on so many levels. I think this is a subject
that is often overlooked and society really isn't aware of the harsh
sides of the family court system because everyone is focused on the
criminal system. I can't wait to read more and see how your story
unfolds. I want more now! I wish you the best with everything and
on your journey and keep the faith that justice and most importantly
GOD will prevail in the end!"
A. Butler, Paralegal

"I absolutely recommend a lot of people read this story because the world we are living in today is very corrupt and you might learn a few things in here that might be beneficial to you!"

-Suki Chrissy, CT

"This book is as entertaining as it is appalling! Aleah's heartfelt account of how she has had to endure corruption at all levels of the judicial system is chilling in its practicality. As Aleah recounts the events that lead to the taking of her small child, it becomes very easy to insert yourself into her shoes and be left to answer the question; "could this happen to me and would I be prepared to deal with it without losing my sanity?

The conduct of the crooked players who have positions of authority involved such as a judge, ACS employees, and the lawyers is shocking, and downright scandalous. At many points in this book I found I needed to remind myself that this was not a bestselling crime novel, but someone's real true life nightmare!"

Jay the Judge, NY

"Finally a book that tells the truth about the distrustfulness of the family court system. Based on a true story and very much mimics the hell I was put through while trying to save my step-daughters from the crazy that was going on. It's like living through the twilight zone but will definitely prepare you for your day in court. Don't wait, get this book. Read it, and read it again... you'll need to if divorce is on the horizon."

"I like/love the fact that Aleah did not give up turning her pain into power. I recommend this book to people who have been in or know someone who has been in this struggle. Hope is never lost.
I gave this book 5 stars cause upon reading this I was educated to the fact of not knowing, I was also a little

lynched by the courts. It took me 10 years in family court to get help. My daughter aged out. I now have my daughter in my life the way it should be"

– Demetrius, Play writer, NY

Amber Alert

A Judge Ordered Kidnapping

Books published by Books HEAL Publishing Inc. a non for profit organization are available at quantity discounts on bulk purchases for educational and fundraising sales and purposes.

Write: Books HEAL Publishing Inc.
P O Box 121070
Brooklyn, NY 11212
Email: BooksHeal@aol.com
For details, please call 516-584-4325

If you like to donate to help save children from abduction by the court system and a life of enslavement and imprisonment:
Make checks payable to HEAL Network Inc.
PO Box 121070
Brooklyn, NY 11212

Paypal: HealMothers@gmail.com
Heal Network Inc is a 501C3 tax exempt organization all donations are tax deductible

9

DEDICATION

This book is dedicated to my son "Doowee."

He was 4 years old when he was illegally and unlawfully stolen from me August 15, 2012 by crime manipulating-corrupt judge Esther Morgenstern who is rigging custody cases in Brooklyn, NY against domestic violence victims, good fathers and destroying their children. His lawyer from Children's Law center was in on the custody rigging scheme, along with anti-social caseworkers from ACS who has a history of fraud, falsifying documents to harm children and protect abusers, and was recently caught again after the murder of 4 year old Myls Dobson. These agencies have done everything to cover up their crime-manipulation; cover-ups of abuse, maltreatment, and endangering children with fraud, maladaptive fake services, and other scams for profit.

Family court, children lawyers, and Administration for Children Services is running Ponzi-scheme style services out the courts. I want my son to know from 2012-2014 I contacted the governor more than once, the DOI twice, the DOJ, the FBI, and so numerous other agencies in regards to his enslavement by this kleptocratic regime publicly pretending to help children and women in need for services to prevent rapes, abuse, and death. Family court is an illusion of safety and the devil has taken over this cultural institution to cause a Holocaust for white children, white mothers, and the destruction of the Black family on American soil

Doowee- I love you so much and not one minute goes by I don't think about you. Until we are together again you will always see me in your dreams like you told me.   To all of the mothers of judicial kidnappings by crime manipulation, I know the everyday terror you feel. My son was captured summer of 2012, my heart although crushed with never stop fighting for our children forever until this racketeering, fake family system of crime manipulation, dehumanization, oppression, and terrorization is abolished.

Dedicated to Ruby Dillon and Lexi Dillon, fighting the prevention of sex trafficking of a little girl taking place in a California courtroom by the crime manipulation tactics are catastrophic. No American child should have to gone through what you are going through. Over 2 million children have suffered in silence. This is so horrendous and monstrous.

Actress Kelly Rutherford- I am crushed that an American Family Court judge and fraudulent system allowed and supported the decision to have your American born children deported out the country.

The stories of our children are terrorizing and I have read over 2000, with over 10,000 more to go of the crimes of these courts. I pray that good American people get involved to bring your children back home.

Melissa Barnett **American Mothers Of Lost Children.**
It's so horrible what brought us together, but I hope we have a bond forever. What we have in common is our children were robbed out of our lives by intentional, calculated, cruel decisions with constant crimes being manipulated to protect pedophiles, abusers, and rapists. American Mothers of Lost Children have helped me tremendously I don't know how I can repay you. You have helped tens of thousands of mothers to try and cope with their kidnapped and incarcerated children suffering from maternal deprivation at the hands of evil family court judges, Gals, ACS/CPS all over the country. I love you lady!

Dedicated to Patrice Lenowitz: - thanks for your support organization "The Nurtured Parent" for mothers and fathers of children captured and imprisoned by the family court system. I love you lady!

___SPECIAL ACKNOWLEDGMENTS___
Thanks to these organizations are doing the work

- ❖ American Mothers Of Lost Children

- ❖ MILDRED MUHAMMAD – After The Trauma

- ❖ NURTURED PARENT

- ❖ FALSELYACCUSEDMOMS.COM

- ❖ CENTER FOR JUDICIAL EXCELLENCE

- ❖ "STOP ABUSE CAMPAIGN"

- ❖ SAFE KIDs INTERNATIONAL

THANKS! *Thank you to all the people that have ever helped me genuinely like Taiwan, and Joan, or helped me virally signing my petition, answering my questions, or sharing information. I'm grateful. I love you, and no matter what I have been through I trust and love God. I want to give special thanks to one of my biggest supporters, protectors, and my best friend. Your genuine love and unconditional love is what kept me going and you and God got me through because my stolen son was your son too. I love you and Poo Poo.*

Thanks for many days of just keeping me uplifted when this criminal acting judge shifted my whole entire life. This ordeal brought us closer together even when judge Morgenstern and her Gestapo tried to frame you with fraud to tear us apart.

Burchell Marcus: Thank you to the big man in Brooklyn. I am forever grateful to you for coming into that wicked family court with me and witnessing the abuse, bullying, and wickedness on my life by a domestic violent judge. You could have been all over the city, but you took your time to take care of, and support me. I will appreciate that forever.

Jason The Judge: Thanks for being a genius a reference and a friend. You are there for me in every possible way you could. As soon as I open my mouth with a need you are rushing to fulfill it. Please don't ever change. You are my brother and I love ya. Tony Herbert: Thanks for trying to help me get this atrocity exposed. Even when we don't always agree you have always been there for me.

Kelly: my new warrior mom who helps with investigations about the pedophilia war in these family courts that are going after women to hurt, rape, and kill their children.

AleahRN

My name is Aleah Holland. I'm a vibrant and vivacious New York City nurse who writes from my heart about my daily, minute-by-minute struggle to regain and maintain peace from the oppressive struggle and strife of a psychotic judge and her cronies gleefully ripping my son out of my life. I was pregnant during the everyday struggle to stop the judge from staging bogus crimes in my home, falsely alleging abuse by me, inventing fake evidence to place criminal charges on me, and creating a fake trial to harm my life, all to steal my son.

Introduction

"The individual is handicapped by coming face-to-face with a conspiracy so monstrous he cannot believe it exists. The American mind simply has not come to a realization of the evil which has been introduced into our midst. It rejects even the assumption that human creatures could espouse a philosophy which must ultimately destroy all that is good and decent. "
The Elks Magazine (August 1956)

I wanted to share my docudrama into an evil system that's enslaving children and mothers for sick kicks and kickbacks. I know the cover is intense the story is extremely passionate and catastrophic. The truth of the story is intensely insane you actually have to speak and meet with the moms and children to believe it. Many mothers have committed suicide as they just could not take it. Many children have committed suicide as they could not bear the torture they were experiencing. The courts are erasing heinous criminal charges and transferring custody to the rapist, abuser, pedophile, sociopath that's unfit to be a parent. The good nurturing loving mothers are being prosecuted if they don't agree with the manipulation of the crimes the court and the system are doing against them. Many moms are blaming themselves for hooking up or marrying a man that they thought was really swell but would torture their children and put them through hell. Even the courts would like us to believe these rapists, pedophiles, and abusers have super powers that could pull the wools over the most brilliant jurist eyes, but this is all lies. Its crime manipulation and it's a handbook and a script for it. They crimes have been exposed. We are coming after their licenses, even the fake ones of the so called experts. We are coming after your funding and God's will this devil's courtdom.

21

We know we have been used as pawns to steal Title IV funding, and the tax payer money flowing through Health and Human Services. We know that CPS all over the country is getting bonuses, and there is a bounty on our children's head if they separate and abduct them out our family. We know about the devised schemes from the "Cash for Kids" you get kickbacks from the institutions you enslave our children in. We also know the "Custody for Cash' crimes you are committing, and even though mainstream media, politicians, FBI, the powers-that-be, and the DOJ are looking the other way, while most are somehow and someway involved and profiting directly the countdown has begun. God will tear this criminal regime down hopefully sooner than later. All the people will rise up and come together.

We know about the intentional mass-child incarceration in foster-care and other systems like insane asylums. Family court is ANTI-Family. Domestic Violence court promotes violence and harm to women, children, and good men. "God will end this "New Holocaust" happening in the domestic violence and family court system! "God knows what is going on?" Judges are telling the public they are for the best interest of our children and secretly for "Best Interest of a Pedophile, Abuser, Sociopath, and Rapists" Judges in these destructive deviant courts.

I want to know how many children have this system destroyed? A few advocates from the 80s have said it could be high as 20 million. That is the said amounts of children to have been wrecked by this system and sentence to a life with a perverted or abusive deviant bum.

Children court ordered and life sentenced to live with psychopaths on purpose using criminal manipulation and enhance interrogation mechanisms.

This book is for the millions of good safe, loving moms all over America paying for supervised visits to see their children like a criminal while the real criminals the rapist, pedophile and violent abuser has full access to the child, continuously hurting and harming the children while the judge, therapist, lawyers, GALs, and Child Protective Services cover-up and dismissing our existence. I feel your pain and suffering This is for children, documented in the millions have been ripped out of the lives of their good loving mothers, and fathers by racketeering CPS workers, lawyers and judges that forced them into foster care, to fund the system while incarcerating the child and imprisoning them for their best interest.

This is for children that were placed in dangerous situations by the people that were supposed to protect and serve them. The children that were tortured and killed after being removed from their parents that may or may not needed just a little help. However, judges like my judge, the devil, evil Esther Morgenstern intentionally lynched their lives and don't mind living with blood on their robes; after all vampires and devils love drinking blood.

I wrote this book for the millions of mother struggling with the betrayal, deception, and desecration of the American court system that was supposed to protect them. It's for mothers, fathers, and children who have judges that are behaving more like crazy terrorist; than protecting the best interest of the children all across America. This is for men like Artemis Schwebel and Kevin Topsey who shared their nightmares with me of how they felt Judge Morgenstern murdered their daughters when she removed them out their lives. Definitely for all women, men, and children that had their families intentionally destroyed by family courts. This book is for the people like me that truly believed that the judge, psychologist, lawyers, and child protective service workers were going to do the right thing, the people that were sworn to protect and serve them; However, I learned that these unscrupulous people would easily burn them and slaughter their family for financial gain. This book is for moms like me and people that truly believed that for the most part America's Family Court system delivered resolutions and justice with the best interest of the child when children are sex crime victims and victims of abuse, or moms would get protection from violence and crimes and got nothing but more tricks, abuse, crimes and their children stolen disguised as justice, and best interest.

I PROMISE TO TELL THE TRUTH

I thought I was finally safe. I finally made it into this domestic violence court. Everyone has been telling me to come here the last few years since my ex had been turning up on the making me vanish for life threats at every opportunity he could get. After years of putting up with his drama, and protecting my psycho ex form the "Black Justice" system I finally took the steps to stop his assault and battering of me, my children, and my family. Well actually his dumb ass attacked me at the police precinct. Lately all he seemed consistent at was doing stupid-nonsensible things.

That pattern of hostile behavior doing horrible things high and a hothead seemed hard for him to break. I was hoping that after a year of being away from him and separated no communication at all he would lighten up with his anger towards me; which seemed to this day to have grown more ferociously.

That was the reason why doing exchange visits with his mother whom he lived with was a little safer object as long as she didn't have her gun. She was a little bit more responsible in public.

The exchanges were always done by other and never I as that was the safety plan and it was working. Someone from my family, not me, would bring my son to exchange custody, but on Christmas 2010 everyone else seemed to have plans. I guess my ex mom did too as he decides he wants to show up and do the exchange with me which was not supposed to be per the custody decree in family court.

Soon as he saw me like a bull on his target he started he would start screaming out in a psychotic insane rage, "Bitch who d*ck you sucking?, You fugging whore, you fugging slut, you fucking slutwhore, you got a disease from the senator, you got a disease from the pastor, you got a disease from god, blah, blah, blah" and on, and on, and on til the break of dawn.

He went into these crazy rants and tirades as usual right in front of our son, in front of my girlfriends, my aunts and uncle that were senior citizen, anybody but a manfriend. If he stalked me and saw a man his size or bigger present he would instantly act like he had sense.

I had cut all communication off from him before he attacked me at the precinct that day. All custody exchanges were done by family, anytime he wanted his son he could have him but he had to have his mother call me, but after she threatened to shoot me and my toddler with a gun I stopped talking with her altogether.

They had to call my older cousin that lived around the block from them and then we started using dad's daycare for pickup and drop off once we got into family court.

Dad and his family had lost all permission to talk to me and that seemed to drive this family that degraded me, smeared me, defamed me, and that betrayed me to hate me even more.

They despised me but went insane when I left their life totally. So at the precinct Christmas 2010 when psycho-dad started going crazy on me I was shocked. The police must've been shocked too because they refuse to get involved. The last 20 years the 67th precinct had become severely incompetent and useless, especially since a cop high on crack shot one of our teenage friends in the neck. The police were more useless then helpful and this was one of the top 10 precincts for racial profiling too.

They invented more crime, and were more of problem then helpful. I guess no cop wanted overtime that day. In the hallway area they were letting bad-dad cut up like a deranged psycho. He was threatening me with physical violence and threatening to harm me. He also was aggressively approaching me with a closed fist as if he was about to punch me. The police did not find any of this illegal. They were smirking, and giggling. The police never helped me I was asking them to help I was afraid to get into a confrontation because I will try and fight back even though I never wanted to be put in a situation like that. I hated that fight or flight response. I live in America not Iraq, Syria, or violent countries warring in Africa.

I hoped the police would protect us especially at the precinct. His rant went on for at least 5 minutes. He would go back outside and come back in and start all over again while the cops looked on laughing

The officer behind the desk told me he can threaten me as long as he did not hit me. He had freedom of speech. I was demanding somebody stop him and escort me outside with my son who he was grabbing on to try and pull out the building.
 The skinny Spanish-lady receptionist jumped in and defended me. Police seemed to think the degradation was extremely funny.

She was scolding him and bedded calmed down then he tried to grab my son and run out the building and use him as a hostage. My son was pushing away from him and screaming for me and he let him go.
.

He continued with his rants rushing towards me frequently as if he was going to punch me as he threaten to punch me in my face. I could not believe the officers were standing around doing nothing and enjoying the dramatically-violent outburst. I pleaded and yelled to the officers, "HELP ME!" They did not rush right in. He was instructed to go outside. With all the violent threats and vulgar epithets the police did not do shet.
I waited inside the precinct scared for about 5 minutes. I asked an officer to walk me outside, but he said he could not leave the desk. As soon as I came outside bad-dad rushed me and started grabbing for my neck his usual attack choke-hold method. I lost the hand of my son trying to deflect his hands off my neck. I was furious my 2 year old son was unattended in the street while his daddy was trying to kill me because he couldn't be with me. My friend ran and got my son. Losing the hand of your child brings a severe type of dark cloud in your heart. I had let him off scott-free in the past when he attacked me, but we were never going to be together ever and this was not the life of abuse for me. Two times in the past he choked my ass unconsciousness and near death. I refused to live like this. After attacking me he ran off after I kept screaming for police and an officer came outside smiling.
The officer told me to go to my girlfriend's house where I was spending Christmas and to call 911 which I did after I was attacked outside the precinct; following the officer instructions after he drove off in a getaway car after I was assaulted and battered which the police could have prevented and did not. I had to do what everyone had been telling me to do from the senator, to neighbors, to family,

and friends, everybody stated I had to press charges and this would finally end.

I tried to make a complaint after calling 911, the police said I had to be beaten and have bruises and injuries for them to file the report, and stop his attacks against me. I Facebook messaged the Commander-In-Chief Of the precinct, Corey Pegues about me being a crime victim, fear I felt, and how his police officers seem to not care that Black children and Black women lives mattered. I told him about the horrific incident and his horrible precinct non-reaction.
How I was viciously attacked in the past and I was finally looking for help but was getting nowhere, and how his precinct had a pattern of downplaying real crime but racial profiling the children in the neighborhood for no crimes, or petty crimes.

I finally had it. The chief of police of the 67th precinct apologized to me and had me meet with detectives later on that week. I told the detectives where the crime took place downstairs, and when asked were there witnesses, I responded, 'yes, all the police officers and the Spanish-looking lady clerk on duty," we all laughed. They offered to drive me home, and I accepted. On the way home there was a 911 call and I went on a high-speed chase to apprehend a suspect we didn't get.

A few weeks later after the holidays I received a call from the police they had arrested him and taken him into custody. I felt bad. I hated having a Black man tied up in this system, but his dumb beanhead ass did it to himself. I gave him so many free passes. The first time he beat me and tried to eat my face off like he was a werewolf I should have had him arrested and put the brutality brakes on. He was on FaceBook and other social media outlets slandering and defaming me every week nonstop for over a year. He was viciously and maliciously sucking all the life out of me and seemed to be enjoying it. Hopefully this would stop all his mean-spirited nonsense.
After the arrest we were ordered to go into Brooklyn's domestic violence court. In front of domestic violence Judge Esther Morgenstern in New York, I put my right hand up.
"I promise to tell the truth, the whole truth, and nothing but the truth so help me God."

To my horror everyone else involved could not stop lying even the Judge was lying. Esther Morgenstern was not there to protect domestic violence victims. She was unusual acting, very cruel, on the side of the bad parent, not the child or victims of domestic violence. I could not believe it. It was a nightmare on Court Street for victims of violence and their children, and their family. No wonder so many mothers and children end up disfigured and dead. From the police to the lawyers, to the judge and in between it seem like no one really cared. Victims and their children were doomed; all these domestic violence employees seemed to care about is conspiring on getting paid off our pain.

No one cared about the best interest of me or my children. The court staff and the judge were just adding fuel to the fire. There were thousands of other mothers saying the exact same thing as me, "Can we please have some protection for me and the children please!" It was so horrifying here. The domestic violence judge was against domestic violence victims and their children.

The judges and this system practice a manipulation of crimes in favor for the abusers and sex offenders to get off of his crimes, torture our children, terrorize moms, and maybe kill us, mom and the children.

It was a domestic violence mill to enslave moms and steal our children. We were slaves against us, even the white mothers were 3/5ths of a human. For the first year in this fake kangaroo court room proceedings, like my ex we talked about sex. The judge wanted to know who I was having sex with the local senator like my ex said, which I felt was irrelevant. I did not care about the porn girls and prostitutes he was having sex with.

Dad had hacked into my computer and hacked all my information and was in my emails regularly. He even wiped one of my main email accounts clean so I would not have all the evidence of his violence against me and the children, but I was ten steps ahead of him I had already backed it up in many other places.

I did not deny the truth of anything that was true. I was a really good individual, still am. I had nothing to hide; as far as the senator goes we were two single adult-consenting individuals.

29

I turned over all my information. The judge ordered seemed very inexperienced at handling the crimes of my ex who had a history of domestic violence, a conviction for a vicious stabbing, and drug selling arrest which I learned from ACS and the courts after I left the relationship.

The process of protecting sex crime victims and victims of domestic violence was elementary, incompetent, and a detriment to the lives of the maternal family they pretended to protect.
Child protective Service in my city was Administration for Children Services (ACS) was a waste of services. They had the most ghettoish, incompetence in child protective services, from their poor and childish documentations techniques displayed in report after reports of severe incompetency. This incompetence which hardly ever had any consequences led to children being endangered, children unsafe, and children maltreated and killed while this child protection agency looked the other way.

Early on my experience ACS was that they were more useless than good. They have been used as a weapon against my family and my children and many others in the community for centuries.
I trusted in the beginning they would do the right thing in their court ordered investigation scheme.

It was obvious they were not entering our home for any knowledge of the abuse, and drug use by bad dad it was more of getting information so that they can use against you and steal our children away. In the past when people would call ACS as retaliation I would have never let them in. Because this was court-ordered by the might judge I let them in but I had to read their reports because they were known for false documenting against good parents of my nonprofit agency HEAL Network Inc. In the past they had consistently false documented against me. That is how I first met the senator. I went to him for their methods of child hurting against me and families of my agency 2 years in the past.

When I reported the ACs worker for false documenting she threatened to beat me up and have me arrested. The ACs worker Samantha had even went to members of my family after I reported her and ordered my senior-senior citizen aunts and uncle to keep my children away from me Christmas of 2009. My family was terrified and my aunt nearly caught a heart attack. What she did as illegal, but that never seemed to stop this children snatching agency. I let them in as the judge ordered but I had to document everything and keep the recorder going. ACS was ruthless.

Now I know why but in the back then I could not understand their method of tearing apart families instead of helping them like they actually can.

Soon as I let them in the same games began. I had to continuously go over their changing stories against me and my family, while they protected the drug-addicted-alcoholic parent with no job and a bad temperament that made him extremely unfit. ACS kept changing his assault and physical attacks on my child as "chastise" in their records. When I told the courts no one listened and it seemed to have made hem outrage and upset, against me.

I was continuously stalked, harassed, and threatened by my ex and the domestic violence judge or no one seemed to care one cent. When the police would respond to my 911 calls they would NOT take a report they would say wait to I go to court. My children were hurt physically ACS or the domestic violence industry did anything to stop it. I was telling everyone that told me to come here how the horror had turned up by ten.

When I would go to court the court would tell me if I felt so much in danger why I didn't call the police. I stated, "I did call the police." The domestic violence judge would badger, yell, and scream at me "the victim" where was the police report? She would imply if I was SO SCARED I would have called the police, as if I did not.
The courts and the system appeared to work hard to protect my attacker and child abuser-ex. Every court date which was weekly, monthly and bi monthly most times, was time taking off of work to get smeared to pieces, and now not only by dad, but now by his lawyer, my baby's lawyer, and the domestic violence judge, while my lawyer stood next to me not really fighting for me like the lawyers do on TV. I would tell everyone that told me to come here what the hell was going on?

31

Everyone that told me to come here seemed in too much disbelief like I was exaggerating the story or now just caught up in their day to day hectic in New York City life-living to care. It was frequently implied that I must of did something wrong to tick the judge off. Everyone told me more advice like, "dress down," "don't look too pretty," "wear suits with skirts to my ankles" Even after I told them hundreds of moms were telling me the same horrific nightmare of what is going on in here, everyone would tell me "they were praying for me."

I had a few family and friends that went to court. I was so grateful for them accompanying me in this torture chamber and to the gas chambers taking place on Court Street. My friend recently shared with me that even now, two years she is still horrified by what she had seen.

A couple of weeks ago she reminded me the very first time the courts conspired to abduct my son and, how they stole him away from me 3 days before Christmas in 2011 for two weeks and how the whole court was heckling and laughing at me when I started to cry. The Last four years every Christmas have been a catastrophe committed on me by this fake 'child protection' fake 'domestic violence' protection agency. Like it's a ritual to severe relationships with children and their moms around Christmas.

That day December 22nd in 2011 same exact day dad tested positive for all kinds of illegal drugs and alcohol my son's lawyer, Genevieve, from The Children Law Center gleefully conspired to invent a fake story about me. I had brought my teenage daughter to help protect me from the fake stories, and how many times I had called the police who refuse to take reports. The judge and lawyers did not care who was there they continued with their child sacrificing, victim harvesting routines.

Genevieve did not give two cents about the safety and security of my son, whom was also her client. When they asked myself 300 times who he wanted to live with, did not matter what environment he was in he would always say he wanted to live with his mommy. Genevieve who liked to smile frequently and creepily while creating false allegations against me kept an arrogant attitude like,

'So what I robbed her son of life with his maternal family, from the mother he was in love with, and endangered him. He is a Black child, most of those kids are psychologically destroyed anyway, and moreover what is she going to do about!'
These people involved in the domestic violence protection project was incompetent, mean-spirited, and evil minded like my ex. I still have nightmares of her saying wicked bad things about me and my family while feeling powerful, pompous and protected by her quasi-judicial immunity. She seemed upset that I reported her negligence, incompetence, and child sacrificing style-of- protection, especially that week of Christmas experience, when she threw her 3 year old client life under the train.
My son's lawyer seemed out of touch with what was morally, humanly, and normally right when representing children. She needed to learn the 4th and 14th amendment of the Constitution while ripping families apart without due process.

She seemed all for the corruption of destroying children and their families. I was horrified and terrified what was happening to me. I cried for a lifetime. Moreover, when I found out this agency had a history of pretending to protect children I was sick. How could this be happening and why isn't anyone or everyone doing something about it.

I came here for help, to resolve the conflict not turn it up ten thousand. What made it even worse was that this lawyer was pregnant while conjuring up schemes to steal my child from me. You could tell she and the domestic violence judge had breakfast or secret meetings together about how they were going to scramble up me and my family so that there would be no more sunny side up days for me or my son. No wonder women especially Black women could not get help from the justice system. Always feels like someone is just trying to make a buck off of us instead of really assisting us. Genevieve's evil ass was coaching my son to say I spent my days playing with guns with my children. 'The registered nurse with the children's foundation to help needy children was now a gun slinger.' That was so evil and nasty of her.

33

Why were they doing this to me? Were their other mothers? Why were the domestic violence judge and the child's lawyer persecuting my family? What kind of scam were they running in here? After the set up during Christmas in 2011 I started questioning hundreds of moms, and then hundreds turned into thousands. I started a weekly Blog talk radio show and the phone lines were filled up. We started weekly meetings and support groups. Other mothers started referring other mothers to me because these custody scams against good mothers have been going on for over a quarter of a century.

I reached out to numerous agencies in New York City and across the country. I started to learn The Children Law Center had a bad really bad reputation and name outside of the industry that created its own hype, gave its self and each other awards while putting children in a life of sex slavery, violence, trafficking, and pornography.

I heard from a few moms that CLC gave Aleister Crowley style protection for children.

I learned it was not only me. Many moms and good dads had their children's life turn to trash under the protection and services of this organization I kept hearing they were good at crime and child sacrificing. At first I did not know what crime manipulation meant, and child sacrifing sounded extreme and horrendous.

 It took me a few months to connect the dots and understand it, and how they were applying it in domestic violence court I soon would learn, and the hard way......... That yes the lawyers for the children were manipulating crime and sacrificing children after they stole my son that August I learned what it meant real quick

There Is A Custody Bait Switch Crime Manipulating Script

I was at a loss when my son's lawyer yelled, "I think my 3 year old client is very credible when he says mommy plays with guns." I almost busted out laughing, if it was not for the fact that she was dead serious about inventing fake crimes on me and sacrificing the maternal life of mommy son along with enslaving him to a bum. God why would this lawyer want to destroy my baby's family? Lord please asks her.

Genevieve said she believed the three-year-old was credible though he was obviously coached into saying mommy played with guns. Genevieve my son's lawyer kept the crime manufacturing coming every court date it seemed to be a different one. After the 1st won which led to the stealing of my son for 2 weeks I never ever trusted them.

The made up very stereotypical- marginalizing crimes against me and my son siblings, such as my oldest son was in a gang, which he was not. My daughter was at risk of dropping out of high school which was the statistics of Black across America, the lawyer made up things about my daughter being in contact with police which was extremely hurtful to me because she had been beaten up in the past and brutalize by a police officer on her way home from school. I had shared that story with ACS how she was assaulted and afraid to go to school and this is how they twisted it, for even more evil.
We came here for serious protection and we were getting slaughtered. All the crimes happening in dads home they would cover it up and bounce it on me and my family. It was false accusation nation taking place against me and other good mom-house-hold headed families.
In the beginning I did give Genevieve the benefit of the doubt and figured she just mixed the "mommy" word up. I knew my son was forced to call his dad's mother, his grandmother mommy too. It never bothered me. My son knew who his real mommy was and always will be.

I was disappointed that they put his father's mom's crimes on me, constantly placing her smoking gun and other crimes on my hands. "Gangster Granny" as we called her did put guns to my baby's head on numerous occasions in the past and no one ever did anything about it. The police said we had to bring them the gun; I spoke to every person in the prison from detectives to sergeants to captains and nothing happen. These incidents were taking place before we even ended up in domestic violence court and from ACs to the police np one wanted to do anything now in 2011 they were using grandma's dramatic outrageous scene-thing against me.
No one in this courtroom from ACS to the police took crime seriously to do anything about it so why were we here?

Every month for 18 months things kept getting stranger and stranger. No protection after, no protection, to being set up in court. It seemed empowering to my abuser to see how much mafia-judicial protection he was getting for his bad criminal-behavior.
After many days off of work, taking off and losing my job, breaking nursing contracts, numerous interruptions in my business for all kinds of nonsensical fake compliance and therapeutic services I had it nothing made sense.

I started reaching out to mothers and every organization that was not in cahoots with them and there are many especially many big ones put in place to silence children and moms.

I had to get to the bottom of this.
I identified something strange things going on in this family-domestic violence industry. I started comparing my notes. At court during my appearances I was congregating with over 20 mothers I met who were labeled "victims" of domestic violence but was left protectionless, and these moms had had custody stolen to a bad dad-criminal who these courts gave all the protection.
Many moms like me had NO or limited contact, and many moms were threatened with contempt or jail if they told about the evil these courts were doing to them and other people. Many moms were put in jail for the taxpayer fun of it without any reason and without no charges moms were detained indefinitely.

How could his be happening to us?

These moms who came years before me and was still stuck in these courts for 5 or more years screaming tears all saying the same exact thing. The courts were more in support for the violent attacker-rapist criminal than their victims.

 Moms were informing that they were bringing bad-dads in under threat of prosecution, but letting them out the back door of the court house, especially rich white men.
Many moms told me this was the court created for men with special privileges and deviant fetishes to hide them from the criminal charges and crime statistics.
Some mothers were ordered into these courts after their children were raped, some beaten, or both mother and child assaulted, that last description was as me. But no criminal action safety plan was in place for dad to be punished for his crimes.
Nothing made any sense in these courts and this system. Was bogus and an illusion of safety and protection.

It took a year after watching the fix and set up to unfold for me to get a grip on at least half of it. Only conclusion I came up with that it was an illusion of justice and these courts were set up to bring moms in and steal our children that's all they were really doing.

Stealing our children and giving them to the abuser, pedophile or rapist they were supposed to protect our children and us from.

They had created an illusion with vendors, and other institutions that were in on the abuse and crime manipulation with them.
I spoke with a few moms that had been working to fight the system from before Claire reeves started 'Mothers Against Sexual Abuse.'

I became Facebook friends with Maralee Mclean author of "Prosecuted but Not Silenced" you can buy it or read the reviews on amazon. She said she was locked up in the system over 25 years ago when she reached out to me in 2014.

These criminalities have been happening for over a quarter of century so far I see.

Nothing still was making sense to me.

I still could not understand how these crimes against mother headed families could turn into such a tragedy and no one was held by any accountability.

This was definitely a satanic system that is why it so was mind-crippling to me. Good people that love God have a strenuous and difficult time understanding evil even if it could kill them.

These courts were straight out of a Tavistock Eugenics experiment and lot more deviant being that they were using CIA torture style techniques and MKUltra programming on moms, children, and families.

I met some mothers who agreed. I started working with other victim/mothers who had been in the game many years before me. These grassroots organizations were trying hard. It seemed obvious most of the major organizations seemed to be in cahoots with the kleptocratic regime.

 I could not believe this hell on earth. It still hurts.

This stuff happed in Nazi Germany not in Brooklyn, New York City.

Everything these moms told me once I stepped foot in this court started playing out right in front of me. We all shared the same handbook-scripted story. It was different lawyers, same firms, same judges, and same script being handed to 'victims' of domestic violence who had children. Things were playing out in front of my face, mother, after mothers, after mothers, victims of domestic violence were having the perpetrator crimes covered up and instantly losing their custody case to the pedophile-dad, batterer-dad, and dads that were convicted rapists.

Some moms had 50/50 custody if they did not bring up the vicious things the days dad had his son or his daughters he could do whatever he wanted to them including rape them..

Hospitals that reported the crimes to police and social services were brought back into court where mom would lose all contact.

You are not supposed to say a word about the rape and abuse on the children. I know the judges and everyone publicly pretend to play

dumb but their nonsensical, confused, lawless lack of knowledge of the law is also scripted trick with many scripts for it.
I always hear the judge needs more training. A 10 year old from the projects are able to make safer, legal, lawful decisions without ever study judicial code of canons or being a jurist

From sea to shining sea no horizon is safe for children or victims in these gas and torture chambers. I heard so may excuses and stories. I remember moms coming to me for help while I was running HEAL. I never believed everything the mothers told me when their children were being stolen ever. I always supported the court system and ACS. I always assumed if the government was trying to take children you're the family must have done something wrong, actually something horrendously wrong.

 I just assumed their story came with a back story that they did not share with me. Moreover, this could NEVER happen to me, not to Miss HEAL in America.
 I was known as a stellar member in my community.

I had political friends. I helped families. I was connected and I was a perfect example of what a good, loving, mother should be and then some.
I did not know these courts and ACS had changed into a child snatching business for the profits it generated for the system. Numerous mothers of all races, from all socioeconomic places were losing custody to unprosecuted-protected criminals by the system under the guise of protection, and best-interest.

The media works closely and hand in hand with blocking out these 200 child abductions a week. You hardly ever hear a story. The 10 O'clock news rather cover robberies in a poverty stricken area night after night instead of juicy stories of criminals going free with full custody because they have money, or willing to work with the system to make money off their daughter or son while they are violently, mentally abusing them and sexually violating and assaulting them. One mom made the news. Maggie a mom made the front page of the New York Post

But Maggie Rhee Karn daughter was still a ghost. She was not allowed to go near her daughter in 3 years if she did she would be arrested. She was court-ordered restricted to one 1 hour a week visit in a supervised center which most mothers in these type of crime manipulating courts are. The dreadful dialogue that moms shared of not seeing their children in years eventually became my story. I had had had custody stolen from me and given to a mentally-unstable man that self-medicated off of street drugs and could not even afford to take care of himself let alone a child or anyone else. He also was not allowed near his first son, so how could he have custody of my son?

Some mothers that were outspoken like me had NO-contact custody decrees. Other mothers had to pay shady inept vending agencies at least $80 per hour to be with their children meeting in bar- parking lots, MacDonald's Drive-thrus or other outrageous expensively weird places for he hour.
The dreadful dialogue that moms shared for over 3 years had finally happened to me. It was such a tragedy.
Mothers are all told the same 'Bait & Switch' custody script. It goes a lot something like this:

- 	They bring you in the Family-domestic violence court thinking that you going to deal with the crimes of dad like his sex abuse the child abuse, child-sex-crimes, the violence against the moms and the children, raping, assaulting, pedophilia whatever crime bad dad is doing on mms and the children

- . They going to assign your child a lawyer and defraud the Title Iv E and Health & Human Services budget if your low income.
- If moms are wealthy they force moms to pay the lawyer around 75000.00/hr. or more until mom is bankrupt , homeless, and in poverty
- In some courts moms get a lawyer to represent her and most times not
- Once there the child's lawyer, the judge, CPS flip all the crimes off of dad, and invent crimes on mom
- The child's lawyer otherwise known as the GAL aka Guardian-Ad-Litem fights vigorously to destroy the only safe parent in the family, in these cases moms.
- The child's lawyer will invent bad stories about good moms by any means necessary, saying it's coming from your child, in many cases saying it comes from a child they never spoke to
- Some babies can't even talk but that does not matter.
- Some children the lawyers never met but that does not matter. They get paid for all of their evil in these courts even if it's invented.
- Every court appearance it's going to be something different manufactured about you, child protective services in these cases are manufacturing things against you too, to steal your child.
- When you prepare yourself to fight the crimes they invented about you from the last court date they come up with another totally different scheme, invention of crimes, tactic, or antic blindsiding you.
- It gets worse and worse most many moms have committed suicide. Or the children were killed.

- In the majority of these cases moms can pay a lawyer hundreds of thousands of dollars and their children get stolen

- This spin-cycle of crime deflection, crime-burying, crime manipulation, exploitation, and corruption, racketeering and fraud will go on, and on and on.
- Many cases your own lawyer is on it too. An experienced lawyer that's not in cahoots will immediately file a federal suit. If your lawyer keeps you here beyond one year they are scamming you too
- The lawyer is going to suggest you are the danger and hardly never ever bring up the rape, abuse or pedophilia about the dad.
- ⬜   Your child is going to be taken from you even on days that dad test positive for illegal drugs and alcohol.
- ⬜   If there is any DNA sexual abuse or violence evidence against dad the courts are going to suppress it and bury it do everything in their scandalous power to cover it.
-

Most mandated reporters are going to see how they are torturing you and still turn a blind eye against you to save their livelihood and even more if they have kids too. They don't want your problems to rub off on them.

- You're going to contact every governmental agency, senator, political, and attorney general supervisory judicial committee and everyone is going to either stone wall you or say the judge is the all-powerful and there is NO WRONG DOING even though crimes against you and your children are occurring
-

The 90 day law will turn it too 5, 10. 15 years. I'm on year 4 so far. In my case with a 3 year old I could be in court for the next 15 years. All of these custody bait and switch games with everyone involved that is profiting and getting overtime blanket-fake statements of Best Interest of the Child" claimed.

- After months and years of these vicious kangaroo proceedings in these torture chambers the judge in cahoots with your child's lawyer, CPS, the therapist everyone who you see is working against you will court order your child to a life of insanity and abuse right in front of you.
- If you cry the judge will order a psych evaluation to one of their inside vendor friends to declare you crazy

- Sentencing your child to a life of nightmares and death while terrorizing moms beyond sense seems to make these people in these courts feel happy, and powerful.
- Domestic Silencing- After stealing your child or children if you say anything they will hold it against you, they will threaten moms, they will put moms in jail, and some moms have been killed for speaking out about the crimes in these court systems.

KLEPTOCRATIC REGIME

- The child's lawyer, your judge, and/or the therapist are all usually friends, AFCC members, or have a relationship outside of this.
- Women judges in these courts are severely demonic, satanic, evil, and give you a false appearance of care, compassion, and understanding
- Many involved have secret relationships with the domestic violence organizations too that do not help you

The professional individuals involved get a joy and happiness from **terrorizing** your family like this while screaming it's in your child's best interest.

They are doing the devils work and seem arrogantly proud.
They enjoy the torture on moms and their children.
They enjoy the pain and suffering
In the situation with domestic violence against mom and sex crimes and assault on the children these court personal know they can make a killing stealing and robbing the system. They enjoy the money they steal from the taxpayers funds to manipulate the system against moms who are domestic violence victims.
They enjoy making moms homeless, oppressed, enslaved, and suicidal all for the best interest of your child

This was straight out of the twilight court zone. I get it this was a complete isolated, calculated, thought out tactic to commit custody bait-and-switches via crime- manipulation tactics.

These witches, I could not believe what was going on, still can't even with all my evidence of their crime manipulation scams and over 2000 moms and children.

After meeting so many mothers, and for 2 years hearing their stories of how they got custody stolen, along with their families and their lives torn apart, I was still disheartened when they finally set up me.

Just something you never think could happen. It seem like for almost 2 years I was just coming to the domestic violence court to play my role of the production of the 'Bait & Switch Script" to make good-safe-fit mommies childless.
Even though I paid close attention to the bad actors in the courtroom and reported all of their bad deeds they committed after that separation of my kids Christmas 2011. It was like it was nothing I could do. I still feel like it was nothing I could do, these people showed how they are powerful and separating children from their mothers they would do to you without a second thought.

The judge and the players in the court seemed to have had role rehearsal right before each of my court dates; craziest thing my lawyer seemed to have been in on it. Knowing all that I know now, she was either in on it playing along to get along or she was severely and grossly incompetent. Nothing she did made sense or did not do. No motions of defense. It was like I took off of work and lost jobs, business relationships, to be shredded to dirt by this domestic violence industry. I was beat up and beat down, all around for over 2 years and then they stole my child. My baby's lawyer deception really hurt me. The judge severing my family felt straight out of slavery. I never felt so betrayed and lifeless. Felt like my child has been killed by the clutches of the people that were supposed to protect him in society.

One Out Of A Million
A SUCCESS STORY

Nelly's Story:
- ❖ Mom Fled A New York City Secret Child Sacrificing Court to France
- ❖ Nelly daughter was being harmed sexually while the courts protected her rapist
- ❖ The courts were manipulating crime and protecting the rapist

Estimated over 20 million children have been harmed by the court ordered abuse physically and sexually over 58,000 children are added unless we end this sadistic practice, put judges and their co-conspirators in jail for their criminal actions.

Nelly knows the nightmare mothers are faced with in these crime manipulating racketeering courts, and have shared her story

Never Without My Daughter

Nelly : Never Without My Daughter

May 27, 2014
From an article in the french daily "Le Télégramme"
© Le Telegramme

Nelly and her daughter are currently living in France. "I gave up my job at the UN in New-York, now I want to live here in Brittany," the mom says. Photo credit: BS

Nelly and her 9 year-old daughter have just started to write a new page of their lives, in France. The mother was charged with international child abduction, the girl threatened with a forced return to her American father's, which she feared. The Rennes Appeals Court decided in their favor in a case that could set a precedent. "There is a very serious risk that the return of the child to the United States could expose her to a mental or physical danger or place her otherwise in an intolerable situation. Therefore it is appropriate, pursuant to Article 13 of the Convention on the Civil Aspects of International Child Abduction, to not order the return of the child". The judgment of the Rennes Appeals Court dated April 22, 2014 was a "liberation" for Nelly, 44, and her daughter, 9 years old. The light out of of an eight year long tunnel, punctuated by "unbearable physical and psychological abuse" and by grueling judicial proceedings in the United States and France.

First complaint when the baby was 18 months old

Everything started out as an "American dream" for Nelly, who had just obtained a French aggregation in English literature. In 1998 she left to New York to pursue research for her Phd in Jewish American literature. She became a translator at the UN and a freelance joumalist for French newspapers. There were the 9/11 attacks in 2001, the US intervention in Iraq in 2003, etc...The daily "L'Humanité" ordered a "series of portraits of protest singers." She interviewed some people and then love at first sight. One of them was "extremely charismatic and seductive, I quickly fell in love." Nelly and the father her daughter got married, but even before the birth of the child, in March 2005, their relationship was deteriorating. This is the beginning of "physical violence and psychological bullying." The couple separated in late 2006, had shared custody in 2007, 20 days per month at the mother's, who lived in Manhattan, and ten days at the father's, in Queens. "From May to June, I noticed something odd in my daughter's behavior, she did not want to go to her dad's, was hiding in the closet... At Christmas 2007, she said she was hurting in her "lune" (child's word for vagina) and more specific things which refer to sexual abuse," says Nelly.

"I saw her suffering"

Mother and child were trapped. They were in distress, all the more so as the ex-husband's new girlfriend became over time also abusive with the child. "She was nice at first, horrible at the end. She shook me, hit me. They told me that it was my mom who put things in my head, to say that I was sad with them" the schoolgirl says. "The Child Protection Services disagreed, obsessed with "parental alienation syndrome," and believed that I was coaching my daughter. I saw her suffer, I could not sleep, I was in terrible state," recalls the mother. "With, on top of it, several charges against me in 2013, $ 250,000 of legal fees (I had to sell my apartment), the situation seemed hopeless, like a downward spiral," Nelly recalls.

Threat of suicide

She returned to France with her daughter in the summer of 2013 in a small town in

Brittany, where the maternal grandparents are living. But during the vacation, the girl talked to a health professional. Horrified, he made a report to the Prosecutor of the Republic of Quimper (five other health professionals, doctors and psychologists, followed suit), and recommended specialized consultations. The girl threatened to commit suicide if she had to return to her father's. The prosecutor asked the mother and daughter to remain in France until the case was investigated. But the father seized a family court under the Hague Convention on international child abduction and got, in the same time, an arrest warrant against the mother, in the State of New-York.

"A sincere and mature child"

In December, a first judge ordered the return of the child to the United States. Nelly appealed. Then, the girl was heard by the Appeals Court on March 26, 2014. The three judges wrote that the child was "a genuine, spontaneous and mature child forcefully expressing her refusal to live with her father who denies her the right to express her feelings". Her point of view was corroborated by testimonies from New York (nanny, psychologist,etc...) and was finally considered. The appellate court noted that "the child has expressed repeatedly and for a long time her discomfort with her father which cannot be reduced to maternal manipulation". This decision opened for Nelly and his daughter a new page in their lives.

"I would like this decision to give hope to other mothers"

BS: - In what state of mind are you one month after the judgment of the Appeals Court?

Nelly: - This judgment is like a rebirth after all those years when I lived only to protect my daughter. It was no life. I always had to be careful to what I said. I still cannot believe it happened actually, I'm still in shock. For eight years, I wondered how she would come out of this, what would be the consequences of this.

BS: - How do you find your daughter now?

Nelly: - She remains extremely fragile but she is participating, always, she always needs to be heard. She is already a feminist! I have a happy little girl again, a little girl who rediscovers life, the joys of being a little girl. I also want to speak out to raise awareness about the "childless mothers," who are deprived of their children. I want to do something for these women. This ruling has made me incredibly happy, but I have a hard time thinking that other women are still in the midst of it, mothers who are willing to sacrifice everything for their children, and now fear that their child could commit suicide. I am basically a feminist. I worked for UN Women. The fact that these mothers are experiencing such unspeakable seems crazy to me, a form of obscurantism. This ruling is a precedent that should be able to give them hope. I am hoping it will bring light onto the current abuse against both children and women.

Where can other mothers flee with their children for safety from America's courts?

ALEAHRN DISCUSSES NYC JUDGE E. MORGENSTERN RIGGING
CUSTODY CASES ■ HER NEW BOOK 'THE RIG ■ HER OPEN LETTER TO MAYOR DE BLASIO
NYC - ACS - FAMILY COURT CORRUPTION AND CHILD ABUSE
2 YEARS SINCE HER SON HAS BEEN KIDNAPPED ■ HOW FRAUD IS RAMPANT IN FAMILY COURT

THE HIDDEN
HOLOCAUST USA
"JAIL JUDGE SALTER AND JUDGE HEALEY
SO LEXI AND THE GREEN GIRLS WILL BE
FREE FROM RAPE ABUSE AND TORTURE"

BREAKING NEWS

ANTI FAMILY COURTS
1 HUB MILLIONS OF CHILDREN
AND FAMILIES DESTROYED

- **LEGION OF**
DOOM!
HOAX DIAGNOSIS AND
JUNK SCIENCE;
SHODDY EXPERTS

BEST INTEREST OF THE
ABUSER AND
PEDOPHILE

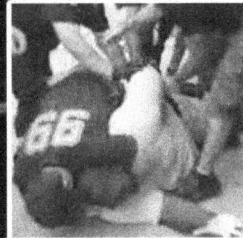

THE FAMILY COURT & CPS
MASSACRE!!!

- FROM THE CRIB TO THE COURT TO THE CRAZY HOUSE
- THE AFCC IS TO FAMILIES ; LIKE THE KKK IS TO BLACKS
- THE SECRET WAR ON WHITE CHILDREN ; NO CHILD IS SAFE!
- REPUBLICANS IMPEACH THESE JUDGES, NOT THE PRESIDENT
- GUANTANAMO BABIES ; MASS INCARCERATION OF CHILDREN
- BABY SAMMY + JUSTINA FREED: MILLIONS MORE TO GO

MOTHERLESS AMERICA

- DEVOTED MOTHERS JAILED, BLACKBALLED, GAGGED,
BLACKLISTED, BLACKMAILED, BY FC JUDICIAL MAFIA
- THE RUTHLESS RIG - MILLIONS OF JOBS CREATED
TO DRIVE THE CUSTODY FOR CASH SCAMS.
NO JUSTICE!! MOM SHOT 13 TIMES ; $2500 BAIL FOR KILLER

WHY BLACKS CAN'T
BREATHE IN AMERICA?

The New Holocaust: The Secret War on
Children & Mothers in Domestic Violence
and Divorce Courts

Mothers are begging for help on death ears. The FBI and the DOJ is looking the other way. Group of journalists, activists, and mothers collectively agreed that even though we have been fighting for 25 years we will never give up. "The Secret War on White Children & Mothers in Domestic Violence & Family Courts in America is a National Emergency,"

Domestic Violence courts are destroying the lives of mothers and their children intentionally and creatively, while looting taxpayers for hundreds of billions of dollars per year in fraudulent protectionless services, while telling the public something different. We have concrete evidence of over twenty years inside America's secret family lawless court system. From sea to shining sea, we have discovered sinister, evil child sex abuse and torture scandals happening every day to boys and girls in these American courts designed for special people. Children like Lexi Dillon just Google the name and the Green Girls sex-enslaving schemes by two different California court judges are terrorizing not only their moms but the witnesses. While Judge Salter in Lexi case is threatening professionals in Lexi case with jail if they don't burn the court transcripts and medical record for almost 2 years we have been looking on in fear.

While a few stories have been published, millions of mothers all across America are being killed out the lives of their children by. Moms getting killed off cause-of- death are not by car accidents or by deaths from cancer, but by family court judge's chicanery, kleptomaniac, and racketeering behavior, which has been increasing over the last 30 years with vengeance on mothers and their children. This is a hidden holocaust happening in these secret courts and it must end.

The immoral incompetence and gross moral turpitude of the thousands of judges involved is unbelievable, monstrous, and frightening. It is an ill of the nation we know as the United States of America. For more obvious reasons, the root of all evil -- that love of money-- has many domestic violence, high conflict, and family court judges running fake protection Ponzi- like schemes on victims of domestic violence and sexually violated or viciously abused children.

Mothers, trying to safeguard their children, are being led into family court under the guise of child protection and domestic violence help, support, and safety. Once there, these mothers are having custody kidjacked from them and given to abusers, child rapists, pedophiles, pornographers, and violent murderers. Children are spending 18 years detained and imprisoned in the unhealthy, traumatizing custody of the family court system guise of "Best Interest of the Child" which is nothing more than a mind-controlling word salad.

Mothers have been jailed and killed trying to protect their children -- and for speaking out.

Other mothers are having their children stolen by ACS, and other child protection service agencies throughout the country for incentives and bonuses.

Mothers, then, have to buy time from family court friend-vendors or beg for an hour a week to see their children that were stolen from them by court orders, or lies, or court mandates lobbied for by unscrupulous social workers. If mothers cannot afford to pay for the supervised visits, services that were designed for criminals, they may not have contact with their children ever again until the child turns 18 years old -- if they still remember their mom; in most cases, children were stolen as infants and toddlers, like author of "Bonshe'a," Coral Anika Theill.

"The New Holocaust" touches on judges behaving unusually, in a cruel manner, and creatively rigging custody cases causing maternal deprivation. Judges knowingly place children in danger with abusers, rapists, and other horrific places in domestic violence courts for the "Best Interest of The Rapist, Abuser, or Pedophile."

This seemed more like the norm then child and mother protection services from over the 2000 cases we interviewed and 10,000 we just did not have resources or time.

When these secret courts were not protecting child sex abusers, and mom-assault and batterers; we learned they spend billions rigging cases against good mothers using antisocial CPS services. CPS received bonuses to separate children from their single-mothers. They had no problem manipulating crimes and inventing fake charges against mothers to keep their child snatching business going. We watched in disgust for almost two years while Judge Joseph Johnston from Massachusetts, behaving viciously and inhumanely, removed a mentally healthy child named Justina Pelletier from her parents and placed her in solitary confinement in an insane asylum. Along with this act of kidnapping, he took custody from her parents and transferred it to Boston's Department of Children and Family Services (DCFS).

Boston DCFS, an alleged child protection agency, "Routinely" places children in "dangerous and unstable situations." says- Washington and Huffington-Post award winning journalist, - Anne Stevenson

From trampling sole custody from good-fit mothers to cutting the souls of children in half and giving it to an abusive or sexually degenerate pedo-dad, divorce courts are showing they are anti-mother, anti-children, and anti-family. Domestic violence courts are the #1 Hub for Serial-killing-families, with a tendency to wipe out mothers lately. The sex abuse scandals being ran out of America's domestic violence and divorce courts are bigger than Jerry Sandusky's, Horace Mann's School for Boys, the Roman Catholic Priests, and the recent England's Rotherham child sex abuse scandal combined.

Some concerned citizens, who seem to be the only ones paying attention, keeping track and acting as an oversight of this family-court atrocity, estimates that it is somewhere around 2-3 million children per year that have been placed into the homes of sexually

deviant and abusive parents intentionally by the family court "legion of doom." No one is keeping track and this number is considered a round-about, closer to the minimum.
The New Holocaust writers reached out to hundreds of good lawyers, who have tried to speak up; some were retaliated against, some disbarred, smeared, and intimidated mafia-style.

All lawyers interviewed have agreed, "This social injustice and human rights issue is prevalent due to the free, unregulated billions in federal taxpayers' money given to the family courts each year. The scheme and protection-scam to keep children enslaved for their entire childhood keeps the funding guaranteed and good. "Shoddy professionals, such as custody evaluators, child lawyers, and social workers that couldn't get work have instantly become millionaires in a few months by sacrificing the lives of women and children.

Advocates like Cindy Dumas, president of "Safe Kids International," have said taking crime away from criminal court and burying it in family court has become the norm and she is hoping to pass "Damon's Law" to keep criminally abusive and sexually deviant dads in criminal court where, hopefully, they will be prosecuted, instead of manipulating the system and placing violent offenders of abuse and rape in family court where their cases are buried, and children and mothers are persecuted, while the abuser is set free with full custody, and bribery benefits.

Many law professors agree with Cindy, and have documented how the "Justice System" Is tampering with crime data as a result of endangering not only mothers and children, but American citizens in the country. Manipulation of crime statistics has become common over the last twenty years in New York City, the model city for the country and the world.

Law Professors in New York, John A. Eternal and Eli B. Silverman, the authors of The Crime Numbers Game: Management by Manipulation (Advances in Police Theory and Practice), have explained that rebranding and upgrading criminals, rapists, and abusers, while preventing crime victims from getting justice is a manipulation of the crime data statistics to make cities and the country appear safer utilizing this corrupt practice.

Due to the data-tampering and falsification of crime statistics, a thousand -- maybe ten thousand or a hundred thousand -- women and children can be raped and abused every year; and we will never know unless they are killed, and maybe not even then, due to the use of data-padding and falsifying tools, which is acknowledged from the heads of states and down.

"There are many different deviant dynamics," says Aleah Holland, veteran registered nurse and author of "A Little Lynched: Amber Alert - A Judge-Ordered Kidnapping;" Aleah's book is a biographical account of her rigged custody case in a Brooklyn, New York domestic violence judge's courtroom.

"I went from a "Little Lynched" to discovering a hidden holocaust. I thought my domestic violence courtroom catastrophe was an isolated incident. I did not know burying the domestic victim and torturing the children was the way DV courts do business. Every mother that I met that was a victim of their abuser was getting screwed and having custody stolen, children taken away, never seeing them again. And paying their rapists and abusers child support along with other illegal federal funds. I learned over 70% of the time the rapist or abuser gets custody.

Other mothers I met at the court had Administration for Children Services (ACS) fighting them to steal custody of their children for no reason except for the ones ACS invented. ACS has a history of eagerly fabricating and falsifying documents to keep the custody-rig going. Just ask "FalselyAccusedMoms.com," another advocacy agency. While I was having my child stolen by domestic violence judge Esther Morgenstern and her legion of doom, I was helping other mothers fight and resume their role in their child's life. A few not many were successful.

If ACS, CPS, and the family courts don't have any children, they will go out of business. Therefore, they create false charges; devastate lives; make children crazy, then medicate them to insanity; they ruin families; detain children in custody like prisoners; and litigate the mom and child to death; or to a nervous breakdown, which then makes mom unfit, and they get to steal custody eventually. They do all these evil tricks with a blank check of tax payer-funded federal resources.

ACS, a replica of numerous CPS agencies, will do many other evil, trickster things to keep their child business booming. Arizona governor, last year, abolished their state CPS services due to blatant oppressive-inhumane corruption. Everyone is in bed together in this family court ACS and CPS Aleister-Crowley style and idea of child protection system. "No horizon is safe," says Holland, who wrote an open letter to New York City Mayor, Bill De Blasio about the systemic scandal in ACS and New York City's family courts.

Melissa Barnett, a child sex abuse advocate from "Mothers of Lost Children," says she personally has met over 10,000 women over the past 7 years experiencing this type of unjust deviance. Mrs. Barnett, along with another child advocate, Connie Valentine, from California Protective Parents Association holds a grassroots conference every year, "The Battered Mothers Custody Conference," which has been trying for nearly 2 decades to bring awareness to the family sex-trafficking- domestic violence support courts.

From Professor Garland Waller, who has been an active voice with numerous media campaigns and produced the documovie "No Way Out But One," to Kathleen Russell, director of "The Center For Judicial Excellence," to Patrice Lenowitz, founder of "The Nurtured Parent and Children Justice Campaign", to her friend-celebrity actress, Kelly Rutherford who has had her American born children deported by a family court, to author of " A Little Lynched" and Registered Nurse, Aleah Holland, they all have agreed that what is going on in America's family court is a tragedy, and a human rights nightmare.

Dangerous pedophiles and criminals should not be protected by the system, which are currently the practices and policies in effect in domestic violence and divorce courts. These courts tell Americans that they are for the best interest of the child; however, their actions show they are protecting the "best interest of the abuser and the pedophile" by any means or manipulation necessary. Family court has become a Borgata. DV courts are functioning like a satanic pedophile ring and kleptocratic regime.

From the yearlong battle and capture of Lexi Dillon to the transferring of custody to a convicted rapist who has sole custody of the three Greens, Sunny Kelley and Lori Handrahan, like Keith Harmon Snow, has these family court cases which go from horrible to hell. Millions of mothers are experiencing this torture in America's family court. It's obscene and a national emergent situation.

The New Holocaust reporters interviewed over 2000 mothers via social media, email, on radio shows like "Untold Horrors of Family Court –ACS-CPS," and in person at court watches across the United States. We also interviewed Mildred Muhammad, ex-wife of the DC sniper who had children kidnapped from her for over 18 months and given to a maniac with the assistance of the family courts, re-branding and upgrading criminal dad under the father's rights program.

We interviewed Doctor Karin Huffer, author of Legal Abuse Syndrome, about her journey in humanizing our judicial and legal systems. We interviewed and met with advocates and journalists, like award-winning television and Huffington Post Journalist, Anne Stevenson, who has been covering these atrocities in Connecticut courts and some others courts on the east coast.

We met with under-funded child abuse advocacy organizations, and spoke with attorney, Colbern Stuart, Esq., who is the president of California Coalition for Families and Children. He is the attorney who launched a class action lawsuit in San Diego, alleging the same malpractice, malevolence, malicious treatment, civil rights violations, racketeering, and oppression in the San Diego courts that's mimicking family courtrooms and appellate courts, and more from Connecticut, to New York, to New Jersey, to California and in between all reporting absolute nightmares and oppression from clients by the court-ordered clutches of the legion of doom. "No horizon is safe," says chief editor Jason Wallace.

Keith Harmon Snow, author and investigative reporter, nailed it in his docureport, "This is 'A Life Sentence'."

"Keith's five month investigation reveals an epidemic of violence and corruption facilitated by Family Courts in the United States. Children all over the United States are being taken from their protective mothers and delivered to abusers. Behind this epidemic of judicial abuse are organized networks involved in racketeering and corruption, channeling and disappearing billions of dollars of U.S. taxpayers' money every year. Insurance companies are being defrauded by medical and mental health professionals rewarded handsomely for producing quack studies that criminalize loving mothers and protect abusive fathers. With clear evidence of racketeering and corruption, high court judges and insider lawyers use and abuse the Family Courts system to destroy protective mothers and deliver life sentences of suffering to innocent children. Rich, poor, middle-class... No child in America is safe." - Keith Harmon Snow

This is definitely a NEW Holocaust. This is not your typical scholarly article, but all profits from the journal goes to saving crime victims from family court, building campaigns, changing legislation to support child crime victims and mothers in the courts, and to "The Children Justice League," and Public Service Announcements against this disturbing social injustice and human atrocity happening to

American single mother parenting families .

This book by Henry Makow opened my eye and helped me understand what is really going on

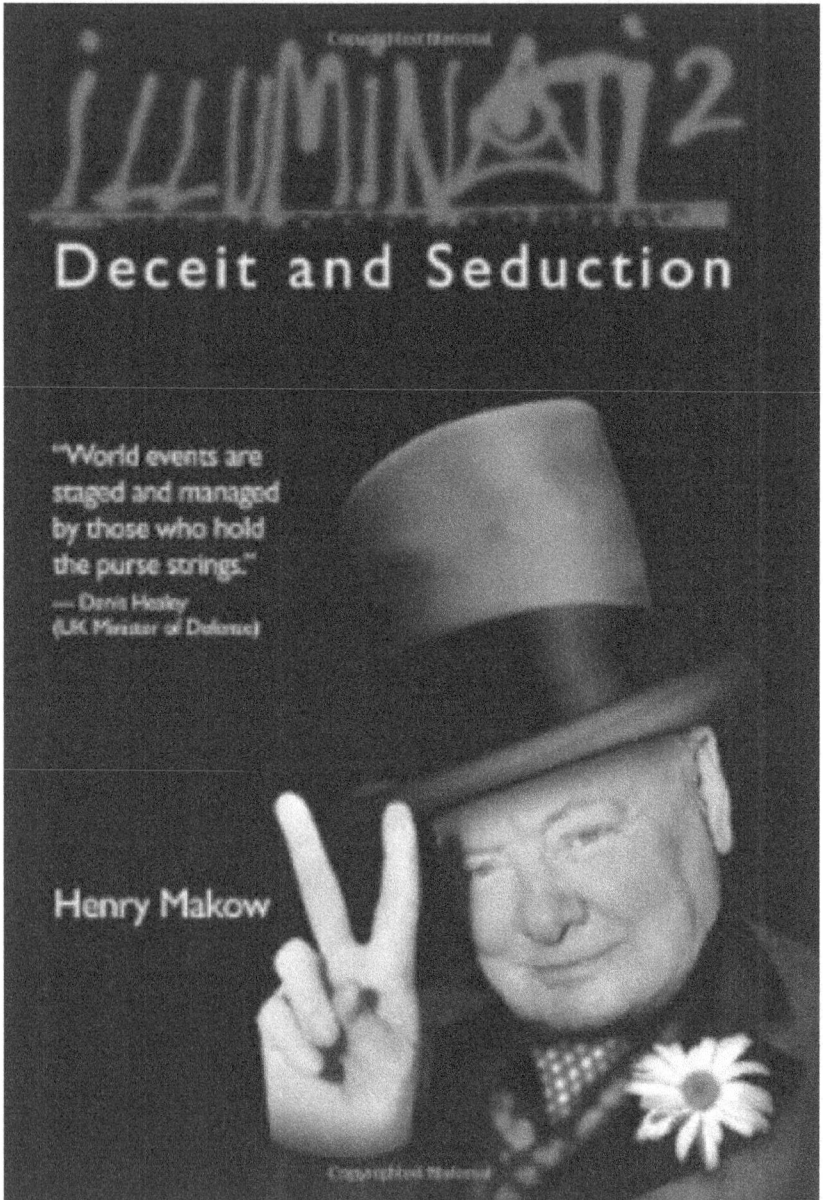

Doing The Devil's Work

Moms that are getting hurt remember everyone involved in these kleptocratic courtrooms are doing the devil's work.

These court people running this corrupt system work for satan. They love giving you devastating information. They pretend to be normal, ethical, moral, and upstanding. They work hard for you to question and even hate God, God's word and God's goodness. They want to destroy this. Hey force your mind every second of the day to be filled with the details of the catastrophe they are creating n you are your children best interest. They force you to look at your problems rather than God. Every day while your children are stolen away you think about how big this problem is and not how big God will be and He will help you beat this tragedy. These sadistic courts makes the evil people appear normal, and successful. They pretend they are better than us, smarter than us, while committing illegal crimes against us that goes against the Geneva Convention rules in war. These courts are immoral. The devil has rewarded them handsomely and they will answer for it. These demons want you to feel defeated know there are a lot of people fighting for you and your lawyer may not be one of them If your lawyer is being quiet he or she is in on it.

It is no longer a secret that these courts are working for the devil. The devil makes everything evil normal. The devil wants to enslave children, women and men. The devil allows rape and torture on women and children normal under the illegal laws they create to justify it. A system working for the devil will allow this type of hell to come to us. This has been an American Nightmare but the darkness is slowly being exposed. The devil is working on a maternal deprivation nation.

Maternal Deprivation Nation

Maternal deprivation leads to mental illness in children, and have even been documented in medicine to cause severe growth and health issues with such diagnosis as "Failure To Thrive"
Basically, a child deprived of a maternal relationship intentionally or unintentionally causes severe health impairments requiring hospitalization for the children exposed to these conditions.

Many of the moms that failed to establish a relationship with the child suffered from some form of mental illness.
However, with judges intentionally separating children from healthy, loving, nurturing mothers, it's causing failing health in American future generation, emotionally, psychologically, and physically. It's been estimated taxpayers pay over 500 billion dollars in mental health and illnesses related top custody cases with children.

I have been a nurse for over 17 years and in my days which I still thought it was this way in 2014, if mothers suffered from mental illness that was NO grounds ever to take her children away from her if they didn't inflict harm, neglect, or maltreatment physically to the child. ACS, nurses, and doctors would work together to locate family members to assist and/or provide the mom with a daily homemaker for up to 12 hours a day or less, a nurse would do a visit every 60 days. If the mom couldn't afford to pay their health insurance or Medicaid would pay. It cost less than $30,000 a year for these services. Stealing children and putting them in the family court/ foster care imprisonment system can cost taxpayers over $1,000,000 a year per child.

This story below tore my heart apart. I learned about a mom suffering from mental illness had her children stolen; instead of ACS and the judge helping her they decided to hurt her similar to the way they did me as a mother and millions of other moms.

"Fausat Ogunbayo and Kelly Rutherford's story which I discovered only after my son was stolen by a custody case that was fixed against me from the beginning.

Knowing that numerous judges in family court are allowing ACS caseworkers and supervisors like Ingrid Williams falsely document mental illness about me; reading this story was a tragic blow to me. In my case, Administration of Children Services did everything they could to intentionally manufacture a mental illness story against me and to steal my son, damage my nursing career, my children's charity and my life forever.

Fausat Ogunbayo Suing City For $900 Trillion For Placing Children In Foster Home

02/07/12 04:35 PM ET

A Staten Island mother is suing the city for a staggering $900 trillion for allegedly wrongfully placing her two sons in foster care and claiming she was mentally unstable.

46-year old Fausat Ogunbayo, who is representing herself, says the Administration for Children's Services's decision to place her children in foster care infringed upon her civil rights and ultimately inflicted "over three years of terror, horror, grievous harm, time lost,

It's a price tag usually reserved for a scene in "=," but a Staten Island mom is suing New York City for $900 trillion, claiming her two sons were wrongly placed in a foster home more than three years ago, SiLive.com reported.

Fausat Ogunbayo, 46, is suing the city and its Administration for Children's Services, claiming that they violated her family's civil rights after removing her kids back in 2008, the report said.

But the city contends that Ogunbayo was mentally unstable and had refused to be treated, the report said, citing court papers. She allegedly suffered from hallucinations, like saying the FBI and Secret Service were trying to take her boys, and would leave them, 10 and 12 at the time, alone while she worked, the report said.

Ogunbayo denied the city's allegations, the report said.

Last month, an appellate court, in a separate legal case, appeared to rule in Ogunbayo's favor. The court vacated a Family Court finding of neglect and reportedly said that there's no evidence supporting the claim that the kids were in "imminent danger" of harm.

The court went on to point out that the kids had a "near-perfect" attendance and were doing well in their studies, the report said. The appellate ruling restored custody to Ogunbayo, who says ACS still refuses to return the children.

The city's law department told SiLive.com that the children remain in ACS custody because the agency has filed a new petition in Family Court."

<-A new petition to destroy this mother and her children and make a profit while doing it.

"God: There are too many of these wicked, nasty ACS, lawyers and judges, please get rid of them."

There are wicked judges like Esther Morgenstern all over America in family courts perpetuating rape, molestation, abuse, torture, maltreatment, neglect, and other vicious horrible and cruel crimes on children.

Under the guise of family court a "New Holocaust" is being created. The war on mothers and children is taking place all over.

I heard of men having difficult times in the courts in having to pay child support, usually after he walked away from the family. I never agreed to any mother using the child as a weapon, and that never happened to any man in my huge family.

However, children that have reported sex crimes, and abuse by pa, are being turned over to the abuser while the courts are not only covering it up, they are aiding, abetting, and protecting the criminal. Not only are they hiding the crimes and throwing it out of court preventing the abuser from ever being prosecuted, they are jailing mothers, gagging them, and ripping the children out of their lives for their major minor age life.

They are denying good mothers visits or forcing them to pay for supervised visits which were set up for the criminal that hurt and abused their children, not good mothers. Mothers also have to pay the sex and child abuser that the courts protect child support. Holly Collins and thousands like her have been lynched by family courts and had to flee to other countries to seek asylum from America's family court. Millions of moms like me were never aware of this family court travesty and have been left beyond perplexed by this perverted, degrading, and depraved family court evil mess.

"God
- EVERYONE told me I would finally be safe.
- EVERYONE told me the stalking would stop.
- EVERYONE told me the abuse would end including the police.
- EVERYONE said it would all end once I finally took action against my abusers violence and craziness towards me and my family by going to the courts.
- EVERYONE told me she would help me and my children.

Everything ended in family court, my life, and my son's maternal family. After entering Brooklyn, New York's Domestic Violence Judge,

Esther Mickey Morgenstern's courtroom; Since my son has been stolen not any of the people that told me to get help has offered any idea of how to free him out of captivity by family court. My children and son's life ended the day judge Morgenstern made that awful decision. I was lynched that August in 2012."
That is the day judge Esther Mickey Morgenstern lynched and burned my entire family. What is going on in ACS and the family/domestic violence court system is unfair, false, deceptive, Un-American, and maladaptive and it is only benefits the crooks I wrote about in this book. Everyone was wrong. Now that my child has been stolen everyone is gone.

Psalm 23:4 "Even though I walk through the darkest valley, I will fear no evil, for you are with me; your rod and your staff, they comfort me"

Mothers who have been jailed for speaking out on the Court ordered
child abuse. Collage from Safe Kids International FaceBook Page

Before I learned all the scams and in these Family & Domestic violence courts, and there are so many. I felt like I was fighting an evil nasty octopus underwater with a Black robe on. Every time I would cut off one tentacle of fraud, another one grew, and I cut off the money tentacle, and the child-sacrificing-tentacle was next, and the crime manipulation-tentacle appeared out of nowhere, then the different local, state, and government levels protecting this family shredding devil, and the AFCC- tentacle, and the thousands of fake-protection organizations-tentacles, and the politicos-tentacles, and the newspapers & media-tentacles that keep all of this silent 24 hours around the clock 7 days a week.
There are so many hidden agencies in our society protecting of this governmental-child-sacrificing-mother-terminating- family destruction operation.

Most reporters I reached out to from the New York Daily News and The New York Times pretended to be interested, and just never called me back again. Or, If they did call back it was to mindfuck me and chuck up everything up as "CUSTODY -BATTLE, CUSTODY-WAR, CUSTODY, CUSTODY, CUSTODY which was key words to DON'T GET INVOLVED. I would call up the newspapers every day and hear the different stories they had to tell me.
I would have friends call and other mothers call or email the reporters.

We would tell the reporter that children were getting raped; they would still say its custody case. I will have to try and explain that rape is not a custody issue it should be a crime, and I was given a million reasons why they should not get involved.

I begged for journalist to just take a look at it. I have sent emails and no responses to it. There are masterminds involved in burying stories like these daily journalist have told me. The newspapers reporters we spoke to always tried to spin our story into a revengeful mom trying to use the newspaper to bring rapist dad, abuser-dad, and murderous-dad harm. They would rather wait until dad with assistance of the secret-courts killed our children before they covered it with inappropriateness and partially; Giving their REMIXED version of the story. I know a few mothers who have had their children enslaved and murdered but the newspaper never blamed the court for it. Had a way of making every court tragedy seem like an incompetent-accident; when moms know it was pure-evil, and malicious.

The major News outlets continuously repelled our stories, the danger we are in, and the importance of our issues, and topics and bumbled, jumbled, and fumbled it all into one nasty word ball of custody issues.

Being a Black woman this was severely offensive to me to see the same nightly and daily 'Poor Black People-Black Family Tragedies', & Black on Black Crime night after night 365 days a year.

There was no airtime hardly ever on the 2000 children being raped by their fathers every week, which was a "white privilege" tragedy, due to so many mothers being terminated, and children being imprisoned.
I know one child Lexi Dillon and her mom Ruby Dillon did make the news out in California. You can Google them. Judge Salter was enslaving Lexi, while aiding and protecting Lexi-rapist dad which in most cases the judge is connect in some improper way such as campaign contributions, they worked together, hang out with bad-dads lawyer, or connected to bad-dads law firm.

"The Family Law Judge at the time, Judge Waltz (the judge prior to Judge Salter), gave sole custody to the father based upon THE FALSE ALLEGATION SCRIPT - Waltz's followed the script that many of these sadistic judges are acting out against mothers"

The crime manipulating SCRIPT is – "*mothers are making false allegations of sexual abuse against the father.*"

Every child should be safe in their home, but that's not the case here. A precious innocent little girl by the name of Lexi is begging for help to get away from her father who is allegedly abusing her. Orange

County, CA Child Protective Services, (C.P.S. also known as D.C.F.), has failed tremendously to protect her from the physical, emotional and sexual abuse she is enduring.

Lexi was taken to the E.R. because she was bleeding and had a suspicious injury. The E.R. Doctor found significant evidence that it was sexual abuse that caused the injuries. Lexi was left in her father's custody, as C.P.S. did not do a thorough investigation, if any at all. Months later Lexi says she can't take it anymore and reports the abuse to a court appointed therapist and the police become involved. Lexi is again returned to her father, who C.P.S. helped get custody of her. August 2012, Lexi reports her father is still abusing her and she continues to beg for help. The police interview her and find her to be so credible that they place her in protective custody. C.P.S. overrides law enforcement and gives Lexi back to her father. November 2012, a reporter reports child abuse and Lexi is again placed in protective custody. Against the wishes and recommendations of the police, C.P.S. again place Lexi back with her father. An innocent child has lost her innocence and the people that are supposed to protect her are putting her in the home with her abuser!

We as Americans need to stand up and protect our children who can't protect themselves! PLEASE sign this petition, so this child can be removed from the abusive home she is in. She deserves to be safe and in a loving home with her Mother, Ruby Dillon.

Ruby Dillon like myself, and millions of other mothers have been BANNED from all access to our children for speaking out against the pedophile rings, sex trafficking, violence, and other heinous crimes moms experienced at the hands of these judges and their co-conspirators in these secret-society courts

I thought about Lexi every day of my life after I learned about her captivity and sex crimes being allowed on her. The judge was preventing her sex offender dad from being prosecuted at all lengths by these courts.

I became familiar with all the mainstream media stall tactics, antics, tricks and art of framing crime to protect the best interest of bad unprosecuted convicts who came with special rich or white privileges, affluenza.

I saw how the media trained people minds to think badly of certain folks and groups which other evil behaving groups that controlled the media was immured too.

The media had me thinking mostly Brown & Blacks committed all the crap and the majority of heinous and violent crimes in America, which is fiction not fact. After being captured in Esther Morgenstern's courtroom I seen what crime manipulation can do to you and how media can mae the reality of what people think about most people.

Media friends informed me that there were special keywords they twist to know when to bury stories like these, and how the cover-ups could go as far up the mainstream media chain to the Hollywood-Pedophile-Rings. I didn't even know about Hollywood pedophile rings. This was way too much for me, but somebody had to do it. It's a documentary 'Open Secret' by Amy Berg, on some of the Hollywood-Pedo-Rings. So, these protection schemes and rings most likely extended to major media outings, to newspapers who have experienced in BLOCKING stories and distracting us from this type of monstrous madness happening to 58,000 children at least a year.

I have friends in media that also verified what I had discovered, and these journalist were even afraid to expose these types of stories, especially since a reporter Martin Burns died August 25, 2013 under suspicious conditions in California after cover the Court-Licensed-Court-Ordered- abuse & CPS-Pedophile-Rings titled, 'Lost-In-The-System'

These crime-manipulating courts seem to have connections in EVERYWHERE and in every industry, especially politically connected to this Family-court tragedy of hurting children. However, one way or another I was going to find out and get to the bottom of this, if I had to go to hell and fight the devil himself. You don't fug with children like this. It's an abomination, and God, and Karma will kill you for it. I have seen it.

I did not understand any of these things until my son was stolen away from me and my family and given to his loser-child abuser dad. His dad could not even afford to take care himself or his other son, so, how could ACS, a lawyer from the children's law center who received a PROMOTION after rigging my case, and a judge allowed him to have full custody of this son. I did not know when I first started writing how fixed and rigged it could get.

People have told me, my now five year old son has been told. "I am dead." Is telling my son I'm dead in his best interest? Is this what judge Morgenstern wanted for my children and family? A Jewish judge, a woman, and a mother should know better. Why was she organizing and designing a Holocaust for me and my BLACK family?

She definitely conjured up a master strategy that led to the tragedy of ending my life that day and my son's for no best interest of any of us. Is this what his lawyer Genevieve from The Children Law Center wanted? Is this what the "Children Law center who are in many states around the country are conjuring up against mothers and children?

My son's lawyer played a major role in falsifying evidence and staging most of the life-crushing making him motherless events,

Is this how "The Children Law Center" is training child law guardians to treat clients? I met thousands of other victims some who had CLC for their child lawyers and they have all said YES.

I know opposing-council who was toxic but also smelled like a vaginal infection wanted, but this is NOT what his bad-dad wanted. Dad was hurting that I didn't want to be with him. But after messing with chicks in the porn industry he could never again be near me. No more excuses for his sad and bad addictions and daily behavior. My savior rescued me.
Bad-destructive-dad wanted to destroy me and cause me pain, since he couldn't get his hands around my throat as usual this was the only way, to kill his own child and choke the life out of him. If he could not have me he would rather see me dead even if he killed his own child in the process

I know Christine dad's snobby, stinky, jealous acting attorney did. Administration FOR Children Services a form of CPS false documenting to STEAL children, really? I struggled with these thoughts for years and kinda hoped it was only happening to me.

I would not want children stolen from their mommies ever, not even all these mothers the judge, child lawyer, dad's lawyer, all the numerous caseworkers I met from ACS that made me their enemy and are mothers or mothers to be.
No child should suffer from intentional maternal deprivation by others. I am broken-hearted times ten million by the American family court and ACS system.
I was broken hearted by this judge. I wanted to hate judge Morgenstern, and I couldn't find it in me. I forgive her for being a demon.

"God knows I cannot hate these demons for being demons, evil are their nature; so, forgive them; for they know not what they do. I forgive myself for trusting them. I forgive myself for believing them, this is what the devil trained them to do. These are the Doomsday Deceivers that hate me because I love you God! -*Mark 13*"

I know now she is not a judge. She is one of the doomsday deceivers the Bible warned us of. I wanted mob boss acting Esther and "La Familia Court" children stealing cartel away from other families, especially Black women and children because we face so much evil as a race. I was familiar with so many oppressive and pipeline to prison prejudice systems set up to mass incarcerate, stop and frisk, our children' and family of their success and dreams. I learned Morgenstern easily destroyed Black women and children's lives one too many times.

At the time I did not know about having judge Morgenstern impeached until recently.

I learned about it when another one of her victims Arty contacted me. He told me the horror about her turning his life into a catastrophe and separating him from his daughter who he loved dearly Leah. So at the time I only asked in my federal claim to have her disbarred for life, with no ability to ever be able to teach at Brooklyn College or anywhere else. They didn't need that type of filth in their curriculum.

I learned she had been stealing black women's children way before I entered her courtroom. I discovered stories on the internet about her judicial misconduct dating back to 2006. One woman talked about giving full custody of her daughter who doctors said had allegedly sexually abused the little girl. Judge Morgenstern gave full custody to the abuser with no contact by the mother initially. Then the woman said if she wanted to see her daughter she had to pay for supervised visits which was unrealistic. Which are visits created for criminals that hurt and abused their kids.
The women had to pay $125/hr. I can't even afford 125/hr to visit my son in a jail like setting with guards watching over us like we committed a crime; the same guard that treats mothers like prisoners and hands their children over to their rapist with a smile.

One woman paid almost $5000 a week for supervised visits while her little son was being raped by pa who picked him up from the visit and was released freely to the rapist by the supervisors at the visitation center. They were doing their job.

Keith Harmon Snow in "A Life Sentence" wrote how one women paid $3900/wk for visit to her child was being raped too by a bad pa being protected by the courts.
I met with a few good men too, all with really bad stories. It was 2 men in the support group "The Nurtured Parent" in New Jersey.

One white man I met from Judge Morgenstern court paid twelve hundred dollars in child support and having a difficult time in her court. I was really sad for him. I told him my story too, but he said, "your son was just stolen from you, I have not seen my son in three years." His lawyer verified the story

She was creating a holocaust we agreed. I started a petition on Change.org. I had a lot of people reaching out to me. Everyone agreed a holocaust was going on in her courtroom. I had been through a really bad experience ten years prior to this with a law enforcement officer. First that and now this! However since that time, I haven't been taken over by the disease of depression. I focused on turning any pain in my life to power.

I wrote a book which at the time was titled, "BEAT". It's about turning pain into power. I beat all the odds, all the evils, and everything that was trying to be done to me by the enemy- the devil. So I knew what I had to do, and eventually I will beat this too while continuing to be the best person God destined me to be.

I've been dealing with demonic people all my life; but she was a different type of demon; an educated demon with probably fifty years of misusing the law. She went to school to hurt people. She was a legal demon that misuses government funds and has agencies assisting her in destroying good families, black women, and children's lives.

A lot of families going into her courtroom were doomed. I spoke to a few of them. I researched for months this new phenomenon of stealing the children of good women and turning them over to the bad parent was the new family court dirty secret, like a new Holocaust taking place. I learned about judge ordered kidnappings. I learned about acceptable court ordered sexual abuse, physical abuse and women that warned the court their abuser could kill her and the kids and they did. I learned how judges robbed children of good mothers and fathers over 2 million over the years.

I had never heard about these things before in my life before entering this monsters court. I had no idea this could go on in an American court, otherwise I would have taken my children and fled for asylum like Holly Collins did. I did not know in the 21st Century a white judge without any reason could just steal a Black woman's baby. I did not know that ACS or any CPS caseworker, who are not nurses or doctors, can diagnose mothers with mental illness, and just steal parent's children for no reasons, other than the lies they invent that do not make sense.

What was even more horrifying was I learned this was going on all over America!
From Holly Collins having to seek asylum in the Netherlands from America's family court; to celebrity "Gossip Girl", Kelly Rutherford having her American born children deported away, and then deported. I was sick. I was pissed. I think I'm still sick and pissed. Angry is not the world for me. I'm ghastly-furiously horrified at this family court and ACS/CPS mess. I really thought mostly all judges were honorable with very few bad apples. I had been in many courts in my life, but I never saw such an evil, dirty, and nasty place as what I witnessed in this perverted domestic violence family court.

I'm still struggling to come to terms with the trickery, quackery, and deceit. I started visiting family court rooms across America. I never saw so much blatant corruption or anything close to being as horrendous in my life. Was there really a new holocaust taking place? As the good saying goes; "All I do know is that truth fears no trial." "God knows the secret plan of the things HE will do with my hand".

So, I will write to save a life. I will be my son's mom and irreplaceable forever. As I continue to fall down this Family Court Rabbit hole more books will unfold

Psalm 23:4 "Even though I walk through the darkest valley, I will fear no evil, for you are with me; your rod and your staff, they comfort me"

I had over 200 FRIVOLOUS ACS visits from 2009 to 2013 while children were being abused, maltreated, and killed.

Administration of Child Services could have prevented 19 child deaths in five years: report

A Brooklyn grand jury slammed the city's Administration of Child Services for ignoring recommendations to improve its practices, leading to the deaths of at least 19 children under its watch. The scathing report was made after 4-year-old Marchella Brett-Pierce's 18-pound body was found beaten, drugged and starved to death by her mother in Sept. 2010.

A few months before my son was enslaved, and abducted I started to catch on to how they were trying to set me up, how they were framing me, and manufacturing crimes against me and my children. I had done court watch for moms in the same child snatching situation. I still cannot accurately describe the distrust and disbelief to the thousandth power that I felt learning about the unlawful, evil, bizarre, and cruel acts taking place within Family-DV court. The crimes by the judge, the crimes by child protective workers, the crimes by lawyers assigned to children, and the spooky-kooky forensic psychologist that mentally and intentionally misdiagnosed and harmed good parents for their own greed, kicks, and kickbacks.

Question America: Corrupt judges are stealing our children away in family courts, some are being incarcerated in foster care, and others placed with mentally abusers, what can we do to stop this?

Later that week after my son was enslaved to this kleptomaniac, Ponzi-style protection institution. I could not stop thinking about ACS caseworker Stacey not only looking like the Coon-ass character Samuel L Jackson played in the "Django" movie, but this facially challenged woman had a ugly heart like him too.

Samuel I Jackson in "Django"

Stacey was one of Morgenstern's main criminal enforcers against good mother and children. She acted like Gestapo. She was grimy, dirty, ugly, nasty Stacey was not only facially challenged she was vicious, and psychotic, very untrustworthy like judge tricky Mickey. Morgenstern, was polluted with corruption and as bad as bad could be when it came to dirty tricks, and she thought she was slick.

She had happily slipped a letter under my door at the address where I actually lived. The letter stated that judge Morgenstern had issued a **warrant** for my arrest and gave my ex abuser an order of protection against me. A warrant was issued for what? My psycho abuser was granted a protective order against me for what?

So not only did Judge Hitler steal my kid, she put a warrant out for my arrest and gave my abuser (who was convicted of stabbing someone viciously) an order of protection against *me*. This could not be happening; my stalker with a protective order? This was an order to kill.
She knew what she was doing. Morgenstern giving this psycho that stabbed someone up in the past and a history of violence a protective order AGAINST me? It was very clear to me what this mobster acting judge was doing; putting a hit out on me. I called my best friend Star so we could cry and laugh about the latest family court corruption. I felt like forty days and forty nights I was trying to stay focused and keep sight of what was really happening; oh it's called "*Judge Ordered Kidnappings*".

While my son was stolen and still not in my custody a year later, I had been doing a lot of research. I learned this was happening to hundreds of thousands of women every year, and had happened to millions all over the country. This was part of the *war on women*. I discovered thousands of videos I watched on YouTube. I discovered "Court Ordered Sex Abuse" Damon's story. Numerous people were hiding and protecting Damon from his dad that would rape him.

The judge ordered Damon to be raped by pa. Pa was going to send Damon to a deprogram camp. In hopes the camp would cover up the sex abuse he put his son through.

Damon went into hiding due to the courts protecting his rapist dad. At 16 years old he married and was emancipated so he no longer had to follow the orders of the family court judge that allowed rape on him by pa. A woman name Kathleen Russell was speaking about the crimes in family court. I was on her website "The Center for Judicial Excellence" There was also an organization called Safe Kids International helping mothers of court ordered sex abuse and violence against children.

One guy, Keith Harmon Snow, "Wrote the Screw the Bitch Manifesto" how family courts were hurting mothers and sentencing them and their children to "A Life Sentence" of horror, pedophilia, and torture. Rich, poor, white, brown, black all mothers were under attack by family courts. There was a really good video documented by Mary Kay called, "*Breaking the Silence: Children Stories.*" There was the Luzerne County case where judges went to jail for running "Cash for Kid" schemes that were similar to the scandals, shenanigans and corruption happening in judge Morgenstern's courtroom. Judge Mark Arthur Ciavarella Jr. and Michael Conahan were the masterminds.

These judges are serving jail terms for their Cash for Kids Scandal. Mark Ciavarella was sentence to 28 years for his part in sentencing children to a life of death for money.

Recently I learned "The Cash for Kids" scheme had been turned into a documentary in movie theaters.
A courageous man named Robert Mays was the director of the film. I want "A Little Lynched" to be a documentary seen in movie theaters too. There were a lot of videos circulating on court crimes and crises, like DivorceCorp, which I only saw the trailer on YouTube. However millions of moms are being robbed of custody by pas that rape, hurt, and kills their children.

Holly Collins who I had never heard of until my son was stolen by judge Morgenstern. Well Holly Collins had fled America to save her children from judges like Esther Morgenstern and was on the FBI wanted list as a fugitive. Amber alerts were issued for Holly; warrants for Holly's arrest were issued for *kidnapping* her own children. When this domestic violence judge stole my child I knew she was really after my heart, soul, mind, and beautiful life. Morgenstern was very jealous and her following me on Twitter confirmed it. When she went home she thought about me.

When this domestic violence judge stole my child she was telling me she did not give a f-ck about the safety, nor security or oppression of my family. She is doing the devil's work and I know that and God knows that too.

When this domestic violence judge (one of only two in the entire borough of Brooklyn) stole my child, I felt she was trying to destroy my spirit. I felt she was telling me that my Black children, my boy child meant nothing to society, and growing up without a mother was an alright thing
I wondered, "how many other women, especially Black women had she done this too?" I felt the humiliation and hate she was trying to displace on me and those women that looked like me.
When this domestic violence judge stole my child, she was trying to kill my faith, my love and my wholehearted belief in GOD. She was trying to tell me my life worth was equivalent to dirt or that of a slave.

In actuality, she only proved that she was a quack whom had a lack of concern and care for Black women and children with crimes of domestic violence committed against them.

She was showing how dirty a lowlife demon she was and how low she could go. She wasn't above the law, she was beneath it; part of the new subculture of hatred, prejudice, and oppressive nasty tactics that was spewing even within the Republican Tea Party. When this domestic violence judge stole my child she tried to destroy me financially and snap me into poverty.

She wanted me *broke*, broke, broken, and broken in mind, broken in spirit, and broken in life full of strife. Shutting my life own as easy as Republicans of congress and speaker of the house shut down the government.

This family court cartel corruptly used federal funding to fight my child away from me like we were not born in the USA. These judges behaving very
Un-American is no new constitutional way. There are no rules, no law, and no order in our family, domestic-violence, divorce, court systems.

   I observed a lot of people turn a blind eye to my plight in exchange for a cut of the action and a check. What made me even more upset was that a lot of the people directly involved with the reprehensible abusive, and hideous fabrications of evidence were mostly Black women. With as many problems as we have in the Black community, for Black women to intentionally falsify, fabricate, and illegally collaborate with a scheme to hurt a Black child, mother or family was unbelievable to me.
For our own people to contribute to this catastrophe was very, very painful to me.

   My child was judge ordered court-napped and I couldn't do snap. I was *lynched*. I was four months pregnant when this lynching happened. It almost snuffed the life out of the son I was carrying.

Things weren't making sense and now I realize they never will. It's beyond baffling but you cannot make sense out of malignant bullshit. *I know now!* This domestic violence judge didn't care about facts, dignity, legitimacy, respect or integrity. She was ruthless. She was part of the problems in the city, not the solutions.

   While I was trying to make sense out of this crap, (this was before I learned about the millions of women and men who were having this happen to them all across the country) I called numerous agencies for help but no one helped me.

I started meeting with mothers whose children were also court-napped from loving nurturing homes by judges and placed in abusive, maladaptive, death traps. We kept coming up with the same unbelievable conclusions; *there was a lot of evil brewing*. I could not entertain the provocateurs and kleptomaniacs anymore. I could not allow these lawless psychos with their fancy degrees try and trick me, disrespect me, and continue to manipulate crime against me. They stole one of my four children thanks to his dad. However, I would no longer allow them to attack or kill any of my other children with their fraudulent – services and lawless rulings. Dad let them use his son like a stick of dynamite against my family. I refused to let these custody war mongers ignite any more fires or drop any more bombs on my children and me.

Enough was enough I could not handle any more of their intentional wars and tragedies against me. It was harmful to the bay living inside of me. invent fake crimes like a sodomite against my other daughter. Everyone was getting paid off me and my children's pain, and paid very well. Judge Judy (the highest paid judge in America because she is smart) further states, "judges decisions could be life threatening". I know firsthand from the trauma and drama my son was placed in. But all too often, justice is denied in family courts largely because of the way we choose our judges in the first place. "Too often, these appointments are based not on ability, and wisdom, but on political expediency, payback, race, gender, and other "politically correct" criteria (such as the case with Judge Esther Morgenstern). That is absurd!" – Judge Judy

I was saddened and shocked learning this judge, the lawyers and everyone that took an oath of office to protect and serve the public under the guidelines of the federal government, ignored and violated human rights along with the constitution of the United States of America. I felt good reeducating myself and updating myself of the laws and constitution I learned in 7th grade from Mr. Schulman. I felt good filing the lawsuit.

I laid out a lot about the judge behaving like Hitler's mother.

How Genevieve from The Children Law Center kept a smiley on her face while she created nasty false statements at my and her child client disgrace. She threw him under the train with no hesitation, and she was pregnant. When I filed the lawsuit she had two lawyers to try and cover up- her malicious misdeeds. She should be disbarred.

She was not a good child's lawyer and should go work with pigs, because that is what she is a pig.

"God now I feel like I insulted pigs"

She was disgusting and despicable. In the "Holland vs. Morgenstern" they even stated on record, that they only stole my child temporarily; and how I could go back inside the gas chambers of dishonorable judge Esther Morgenstern courtroom and fight for my son back. Was this an evil game?

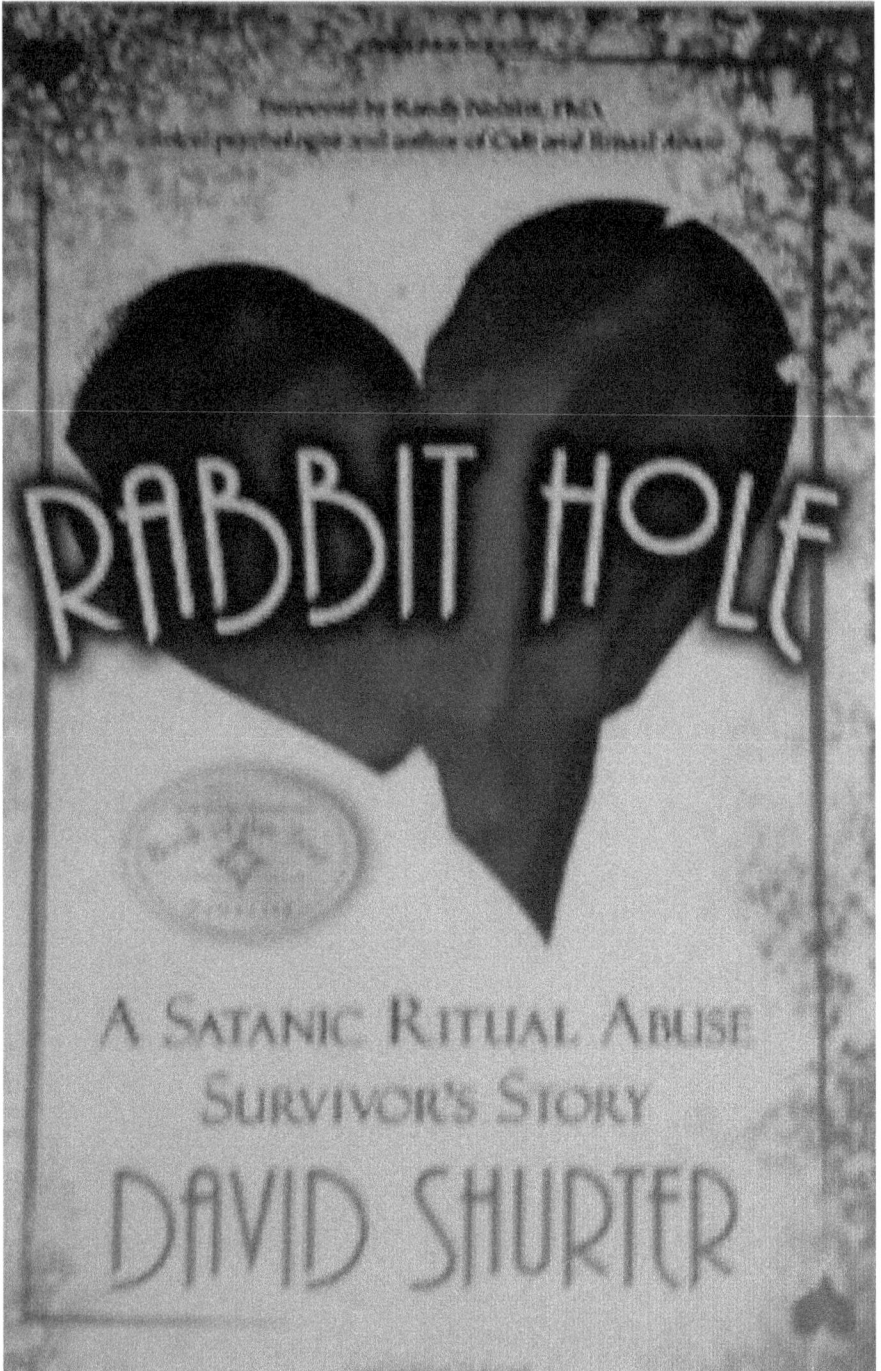

RABBIT HOLE

A SATANIC RITUAL ABUSE
SURVIVOR'S STORY

DAVID SHURTER

Down The Domestic Violence Rabbit-Hole

A lot of child sex abuse survivors are writing books being that the system has tried endlessly to bury them and their voices relentlessly. This scandal is worse than the Roman Catholic church, Penn state, Boystown, the 1200 boys raped in the Texas juvenile detention center put together.

You can go to amazon there are thousands of book on incest, ritual sex abuse, and the crimes of these courts. So funny when you search for these titles lot of illuminati books The media and major newspapers have joined forces too in many cases to make sure these stories never get through.
I was tired of going to dead end, do nothing agencies. I decided to document this story to at least help one family.

Nobody believes what is going and many pretend they don't understand or believe because they are part of the organized crime manipulating system. A lot of times that is part of the public pretending. Many politicians get huge campaign contributions from these sadistic losers.
I remember I went to one Black organization in person and the woman I told my story to, looked at me as if I were lying. She put her hand up two inches from my face and said, "*Hold up!*" she shouted. She rudely blurted out, "*I do not believe a word you are saying; a judge can't just steal your child away from you for no reason. You must have done something wrong.*"

She continued to say, "A judge definitely cannot give him [my son] to a convicted drug addict, an alcoholic who tested positive every day with a current open criminal case for abuse, and all these things you are claiming". She told me flat out, "*you are making no sense.*" She told me to get the transcripts and come back because she didn't believe jack I had to say. It took a few months to get all the transcripts. It also took over one thousand dollars which I really didn't have, but I spent it instead of paying rent. *Here comes the domino effect.*

I really didn't like the way the lady behaved at that Black national organization so I decided not to go back. I had spoken to what felt like a few hundred more people from the courts; all directing me to hundreds of do nothing agencies. Every day was a dead end until I decided to end it all.

During the time period leading up to and after the kidnapping of my son, I felt severely distressed, depressed, and without rest. It was like that mean lady said at the Black organization in Harlem; this did not make any sense. None of this made sense. Since it was senseless I had to take all my energy out of it. I had to reclaim my peace and serenity and let that monster of a judge "Manson Morgenstern" alone.

She had to know she behaved criminally and that it made no sense even to her, but these were the illegal cards that she happily dealt. She was not honorable. She was disgusting. She was nasty. She was a very evil, demon like woman. Every time I thought about her, Hitler popped into my head. I knew he must have been raised by a woman like judge Morgenstern. She definitely could have been Hitler's mother, delivering evil with a pretty face, a smirk and smile. I refused to let this demonic judge trap me up in the cages, tricks, and traps she was trying to wrap my life up in. She was using one child to bully me and destroy the rest of my family.

First, I had to get this illegal warrant off of me. So on August 21, 2012 I thanked Judge Henry. She dismissed the malicious warrant that was placed on me by Judge Morgenstern.

Judge Henry had also assigned me a lawyer whom judge Morgenstern refused me to have while allowing the father's lawyer Christine, child careless crooked lawyer Genevieve and ACS antisocial uncivilized

Gestapo to invent, forge and falsify evidence against me and my family.

I wished Judge Henry would've revoked the bogus protective order that judge Morgenstern had given my abuser too, but she did not. Judges in these courts don't go against each other even when they know their colleagues are committing crimes.

The hit that judge tricky Mickey Morgenstern had placed on me is still in effect to this day. The unlawful order expires July 2014. Months later I read the transcript on July 18, 2012 when I informed them I was leaving court due to bleeding and being pregnant, well that same day Esther decided to hold a kangaroo court without me having a lawyer.

She had been denying me a lawyer and forcing me to represent myself for almost a year. So at this "mock" trial (after my abuser had just been arrested again 3 weeks prior for abusing a child and with a new open criminal case) judge Morgenstern decided to create charges against me. I guess to level the playing field. She had my druggie, alcoholic, unemployed, child neglecting abuser testify against me. She then prosecuted and convicted me. She gave my psychotic abusive ex an order of protection; get it? I knew exactly what was happening. Can someone say mafia hit?

From the moment we entered family court, my ex had three separate open criminal cases; two of which judge Morgenstern transferred from criminal court and into her court where they did not belong.

I learned she did that on other cases too. It's called corruption and scandal. She would have the cases transferred into her court where she would intentionally bury them and dismiss the charges. I didn't know if she was taking a payoff or if she was having sex with my ex. I didn't know what kind of kickbacks she was collecting.

She was definitely taking unlawfully biased risks. These cases are called *fixed*. Was it just for kicks? Her behavior was similar to sociopaths. I knew judges in the past that went to jail for fixing cases in the very same building she sat her crooked ass. My four year old told the police from the 67th precinct about the abuse and the attack. He told everyone at daycare about his dad's whacky, cracky, tacky behavior. However, this time Genevieve didn't think he was credible I guess. He was credible at the age of three when she was fabricating evidence against me.

When he talked about witnessing his dad attack his sister and how it made him sad, he wasn't credible then. I thought to myself,

"He is older now, I don't know why. She thought he was credible when he was three and said his mother (the Registered Nurse for fifteen years that has a children's foundation) plays with him with real guns, yet isn't credible older at this time when witnessing his father attacking his sister."

It was clear he was credible when they coached him to say things. She knew giving my stalking psycho ex an order of protection was saying he could beat me, hurt me, or kill me and he was protected by her.

"Aha! Aha! Light bulbs are going on everywhere. I finally get what's taking place here. This is what demons do. There is no truth in their evil. Nothing they do makes sense."

They are ruthless, soulless, demons! They will never admit to their sociopath, psychotic ways. They keep up their injurious, harmful wrath until somebody exposes their asses, and they still will never admit to their wrong doing. They live to perform badly. They are usually narcissistic sociopaths, and live for insanity. There's usually a lot of money being passed under the table, and for the root to all this evil, they will vilify you and try to make you unstable.

I contacted news agencies, but no one responded. I remember a local news station had come out the first time judge Morgenstern stole my son away from me three days before Christmas of 2011. Brooklyn channel 12 News' Crystal Walker came and interviewed me with Tony Herbert when my son was first stolen but the news piece never aired. She said the courts were closed and they couldn't confirm the story so they couldn't air it.

I contacted them again but they didn't care. Nobody cared because it wasn't their child, *yet*!
After meeting with, talking to, and reading stories of hundreds of moms, all have said the same thing; mainstream media didn't give them the time of day, and were happy to see celebrity Kelly Rutherford from the television show, "*Gossip Girl*", get the coverage.

For months my heart felt like it was suffocated, wrapped in a plastic bag and chained down from beating.
I felt lynched, but I had to be strong for God and my other kids. I loved God yet I felt powerless, helpless, and hopeless.

I believed God would help me to keep my strength up, especially since I was pregnant. Since I loved God so much, I asked him for strength. How could I go on when I was just lynched? I wrote out my feelings every second of every hour of every day. I felt better this way. It helped me. After writing thousands of emails to myself, searching everywhere for help, expressing my feelings, and trying to tell my story, it was clear NOBODY CARED about my son!. It seemed like the only one that was listening to me was God.

So instead of writing everywhere and begging for help, I decided to be still, keep calm, keep my thoughts, and keep the peace inside myself even as the war raged against me and my family.

I continued to gather transcripts, and documents like the false reports that the corrupt asinine ACS workers had forged about me. But I designated a day in the week to deal with this deception and deceit, Thursday.

One day of dealing with distressing mess and then a four day weekend until Tuesday. On Thursday of the following week, I decided to file a federal lawsuit. I decided to write up a federal claim. I am not a lawyer nor do I pretend to be one in real life or on TV, however I know the constitution, I know how to read, and I know how to research. Google was a big help. Years ago I would have to go to the library for hours a day and do all the research I could do to get the most accurate information I could get from Google.

First, I researched numerous lawsuits against judges, Administration for Children Services, lawless lawyers and so on. I couldn't believe how many lawsuits there were. There were millions of lawsuits to choose from.
It disturbed me to see how many people's lives they destroyed or injured before mine. After researching, I filed my complaint prose in the Brooklyn Federal court. I decided to sue for me and everybody whose lives they'd besieged with their wicked, fraudulent family domestic violence court protection, best interest of the child garbage. I filed a $999 trillion dollar lawsuit.

My federal claim was filed September 28, 2012 *"Holland vs. Morgenstern."*

I missed Constitution Day which is September 17.
I was tired and not feeling good
While looking for an attorney to accept my case, I decided to file suit against all subjects involved in order to expose the maliciously cruel, calculated, collusion, malicious unusual, and evil heinous racketeering style corruptive abuse taking place in domestic violence and family court. When asked by the clerk what amount I wanted to sue for, I figured due to this "New Holocaust" being created, all the moms and children they castrated, the pas the aided and abetted and my precious baby being priceless, I stated $999 trillion dollars. The clerk said so add it in.

"Holland vs. Morgenstern"

Holland vs. Morgenstern was always Esther Morgenstern (the judge) vs. Holland, Genevieve Tahang-Behan (the son's lawyer) from "The Children Law Center" vs. Holland, A clan of corrupt crazy child protective workers from the Administration for Children Services vs.

Holland and the father's lawyer vs. Holland! ACS responded with the DeShaney vs. Winnebago. I stated how I was disgusted by the domestic violence judge, ACS, my son's lawyer, and all the other perps involved in the racketeering and kidnapping cover up of my four year old son Doowee.

The judge and the child lawyers pleaded they had quasi-judicial immunity and immunity. They used the eleventh amendment as their dispute for their hatefulness, viciousness, and venom towards me and my children. Basically stating, no matter how wicked, dirty, nasty, ruthless or illegal their breach of law was, and unconscionable their criminality is, they were immune from punishment.

I write from my heart about how ACS/CPS and family courts are abducting children, enslaving them and wrecking women by design. Even if you are an awesome mother Esther Morgenstern's courtroom will make your child motherless like she did to me and others. I began a yearlong investigation which I later learned; this is happening to millions of parents especially to mothers all over America. There is a new incentive to give full custody to dad even if pa is a molester, sodomizer, rapist, abuser, or murderer. I learned this in one year leading me to look back and think my lawyer at the time Louisa was a piece of crap, and most likely was in on it. Lawyers can make millions in a few months if they go along with the corruption in family courts, and many are signing up.

Louisa had allowed my son to be stolen the first time on December 22, 2011. She did nothing to stop my 3 year old son from being swindled out of our life. He was hustled over to the people that was abusing him, neglecting him, maltreating him, and putting guns to his head all with the protection of child services and judge Morgenstern. It was like the family court crew was setting my family up for tragedy; for something even death to happen to the children or me. Knowing what I know now about these family court crimes and kidnappings, I look back I believe Louisa was either in on it, or she was just extremely incompetent.

"If you are not part of the solution, you are part of the problem." - *Eldridge Cleaver*

So back to manic Morgenstern vs. Holland; after lousy lawyer Louisa sold me and my children out too, I was forced to show up without a lawyer while these demons devoured me and fabricated crimes to charge me with at every court date.

When Honorable judge Patricia Henry, well honorable at the time to me, I don't trust anybody in that building anymore, well judge Henry ordered an attorney for me on August 21, 2012, judge Morgenstern continued to defy the order.

Morgenstern wanted to exploit, extort, and financially destruct my children and me. She wanted me to pay hundreds of thousands for a lawyer to deal with her vile and evil orders. Truthfully, Morgenstern was lawless and a lowlife judge. I was embarrassed that she was a judge in my home state. I was appalled by her and ashamed for her. January 10, 2013 two days after a complicated C-section (where I almost died) she FINALIZED the corrupt and crooked custody order, which was always final from August 15, 2012 but they use trickery in paperwork to make it look like its temporary so you have a more lies and run around in appellate court town.

I know dad's mom was happy. He didn't want full custody it was his mom taking care of my son and fraudulently getting benefits and collecting taxes on. My son was a meal ticket. Last time I saw his mom in Morgenstern's courtroom she was poking out her tongue sticking her middle finger up yelling "na-na-na na- na na, we going to steal your son you f-cking bitch. She kept repeating it." I got a call today that she died. Only a year later; that was quick, Karma aint nothing to play with. Wow! Life: Pa stole my son from me and his mother now was stolen from him. As an only child I knew pa was feeling it. Back to the psychosis in these crime manipulating courts, I know it will haunt me for the rest of my life. I will never look at any judge the same, even though I have been in normal courtrooms, with normal judges before. Getting back to the 999 trillion dollar lawsuit I filed and then walk away from, well waddled I was 8 months pregnant and didn't want to deal with it.;

After I brought claim against these parties for being demons, the judge, my son's lawyer, and child protective workers were all given lawyers. Genevieve had two lawyers from the Children's Law Center represent her. (most likely at tax payers' expense) "I wanted to see the financial records." Never did I think to fight these legal demons prose that made no sense. Unfortunately the lawyer I was talking with was affected by Hurricane Sandy a month after I filed the federal claim and could not represent me. I never planned on fighting this alone (and still don't), however September 26, 2012, I had documented the abuse, and the crimes the best way I could as a registered nurse 8 months pregnant sitting at times for over twenty hours studying the laws to bring my child sacrificing-crime manipulating defendants to trial I wanted them all to lose their license to practice anything ever again. These filthy demonic dirtbags should not be allowed near pigs let alone children and humans. Their whole system is fraud, nothing more than a kleptocratic-racketeering ring being ran out the courts.

The more I studied the more I learned about the truth of this holocaust and decided I need time off from the madness. After speaking to another lawyer, he told me, " sue their asses later on take care of myself, you are pregnant, don't worry about this right now, you can always sue their asses again!" He was right. I was not going to spend the next 10 and 14 years fighting with family courts and their lies about what the best interest of my child were, and a scorned ex love that was still abusing his child.

My child was in love with his mother, and still is. He told everyone in his fathers' presence, at his school, and everywhere else that he went that he loves his mother and that is who he wants to live with to this day. How could they do this to him? How could his lawyer Genevieve do this to him? I learned millions of mothers all over America are mourning for their children in the same way. Their children were kidnapped by family courts and given sole custody to unfit, misfits, that abuse and have sex with their children. They are putting mothers in jail. They are threatening them with jail and gagging them if they think about talking, and they are sealing the family court records to cover-up what they are doing.

"Don't you good Americans dare believe for one second that they are sealing the records to protect nothing other than their court crimes against humanity. These scandalous lowlifes don't give a dam about a child's best interest .I learned good fathers are losing custody too especially in Morgenstern's courtroom. Fathers like Artemis Schwebel, whom monster Morgenstern stole his daughter away from, and Kevin Topsey too. Some moms and a few good dads will continue this merciless fight with family court, until their children age out. I will write books, columns, and documentaries about their crimes and torts while the tax paid family court system are paid to cover-up the cover-ups. So that is why I gave up the "Holland vs. Morgenstern" lawsuit. I can't pursue lawless people. It was stressful to me, to my baby, and my life. I have a beautiful life, wonderful children and fabulous family. The lawsuit had me dealing daily with vile, evil, lowlife, lawless, satanic, demons.

When I put it in God's hands, He decided writing books was a better plan. Write and take all the money from the books and put it into "*Project: Safe Kids!*" It was an awesome idea then and that is the only plan I follow now. Was this how family courts really worked in America? I'm afraid so. I met some women fighting for 10 years. Her child aged out that's how the custody war ended. I met a man that was fighting for 15 years. His name was Sonny. His children had aged out too, but still were pursuing the federal lawsuit for the violations on his life when his children were minors. So I was to go back into this racist, sadistic judge court where they planted guns in my home but covered up the murder suicide attempt at dad's home, where guns were put to my toddler son's head, and by the way this is who has full custody of my stolen son. I can go back in judge Morgenstern's courtroom where drugs were planted in my home, but dad could test positive for illegal drugs and alcohol all day; where they just dismissed every positive drug test for six months, until judge Morgenstern suspended the daily testing and never tested again.

I could go back into her court where they placed rape charges (which they invented after 3 years of being there) on my remarkable daughter, but dad new pimp career and porn girlfriend wasn't of any concern to them. I could not go back into judge Morgenstern's court room where they planted evidence in my home and buried the father's multiple arrests; I could not go back in judge Morgenstern's Kangaroo court. It was a bad circus full of dirty tricks. I realized it takes two to fight. They had already illegally stolen my son and I could spend the rest of my life fighting them to get him back, which was whack. I will always be his mother. I could not spend the rest of my life fighting. I had to protect me and my other children they were coming after. I almost lost my new baby on July 18, 2012. Justice who became the light of my life was born January 08, 2013, same exact day as his brother that was stolen away.

"God has miracle ways of helping to heal heartache and pain. I could not allow them to plant anymore vile, nastiness, and disgusting fake evidence in my home. I could not allow ACS to torment, and torture my other children nor abuse and maltreat them any longer. I couldn't watch while they allowed my ex, to torment and torture Doowee. I could not go back into that domestic violence gas chamber where the judge and Gestapo invented crimes and malicious attacks while accusing my other children of abuse; while the real abusers' criminal activities were buried.

"The actual, yes the main person that started this entire war against me was dad's mom and now she is dead." I heard she died a painful death." I was not going back in domestic violence court. I wasn't going back into any court, well criminal court where I had to deal with dad hallucinations, creation of fake conversations and fake criminal charges. God: I need to maintain the pieces of my life, avoid the stress, and learn how to live one child less, which feels like every day I'm experiencing a horrible death. It was obvious he was going to abuse his child with protection of these legal evil clowns. I tapped out. As I continue to fall down this family court rabbit-hole more books will unfold. I spend a lot of time enjoying my new son. Justice was born the exact same day as the son that stolen from me. Justice and Howard share the same birthday

War on Mothers & Children

The war on children and moms is leading us into a secret holocaust. A holocaust created for greed and hatred. It's desecrated our social and community institutions that we are supposed to be safe in

The war on mothers and children is taking place in every secret court room in America. No horizon is safe for children and women in America anymore. Rape and abuse of women and children is being manipulated in these secret courts with millions of employees of the court and scheme in cahoots with the system against the victims.

These Domestic Violence systems set up as Societies "GO TO for PROTECTION is proving themselves to be Ponzi-scamish and crime-manipulating organizations. My abuser like most moms was never prosecuted for his crimes and was able to steal my child with the assistance of an entire system that's protecting criminals.

Mom thinking they would receive help was intentionally duped. They had due process stolen from them when their children were stolen and their abuser received special processes by the people in the court that protect his every criminal step.
Special processes to actually it hide sex abuse, child porn, child trafficking of children to hide incest, hide pedophilia, hide rape against women and hide rape against children was in place to cover it, monitor it every step of the way.

These Domestic violence courts seem to be a management tool to hinder protection and keep disorder ongoing. Moms end up in jail or dead if they say too much against the courts.

I don't know why it is going on but something terribly evil and sadistic is happening. The court process aids and abets the violent psycho-rapist-dads and abuse, beat-up, beat-down and further violate the lives, liberty, and justice of women and children.

These courts use Child Protective Services; here in New York City ours is called ACS, 'Administration for Children Services.' ACS are in on the protection scam of children, and also aide bad dads that hurt rape, molest, and viciously assault their children into obtaining custody while deliberately going against safe-fit mothers to steal away custody

ACS is the eyes, ears, and voice for the mother, father, and child in these courts. As I didn't know how the system worked exactly before my catastrophic custody case.

These systems are embedded in the American Family/Domestic Violence court JUSTICE system as a place for protection, with over a million children harmed have proven to be a scam. You can GooGle how many scams have led to the deaths of children in these kleptocratic-ponzi-protection systems.

I was horrified that these courts that everyone told me to allow in helping me achieve peace, and safety enslaved me into a life of hell. Do the politicians that told me to get help, the police that told me to get help, and my health professional friends and family know that these systems protect rapists, and child abusers? Do everyone that told me to go to these courts for help know how they are planting crimes and moms and erasing crimes off abusers and rapists to steal hey know they practice "crime manipulation and give our children to sexual predators?

The public pretenders in these courtrooms like my judge, the lawyers, GALS, evaluators, and social workers are practicing trickery and disgrace.

People told me that these courts were the solution to my ex victimizing intrusions on my life. I thought Domestic Violence court was the answer to end my batterer's abuse against the children and me like everyone from the local senator's office to the police, and everyone in society told me. My truth and research is that Family Court, Domestic Violence organizations, ACS/CPS, and many and business to business tied to family court are built on fraud, racketeering, and crime manipulation

These are Kleptocratic Institutions with an ILLUSION OF SAFTEY embedded into society while trying to abstract all the resource funding, tax funding, and life savings from every family, they have an extraction strategy "extraction institutions."

"Extraction Institutions" - Their purpose is to wring as many-much resources/property from the people as possible while keeping power to a narrow elite.

MIT and Harvard "think tanks" have formulated that the reason behind wealth imbued and poverty stricken nations hinges entirely upon the man-made political AND economic institutions, both codependent and driving the other.

I WANT THE WORLD TO KNOW WHAT THEY DID TO MY SON
ALEAH HOLLAND Is THE JUDGE On Drugs?

Our Family Court and CPS systems are the Bernie Madoff-Ponzi scam, Aleister Crowley-child sacrificing, Jerry Sandusky-pedophilia protection, Son-of-Sam-Serial family killing organizations created for the best interest of children, just a word salad.

Anti-Family- Domestic Violence, and other equity courts seem to be where all the destruction and disorder in America is rooted from. Fake solutions, fake help, fake services, that come with hefty prices for fake professionals operating in these fake courts of law

As a nurse being around people that save lives for over 17 years I have been horrified by what I discovered. Its so monstrous after hearing the stories from over 3000 cases did I start to believe it, and the advocate had over 7000 names of other mothers who experienced this same evil child protection, domestic violence protection game.

In the past I would have been quick to recommend domestic violence court and DV organizations as a safe haven. Now, I know no horizon is safe.

I will NEVER in my life tell a woman abused by her mate or husband to go to any domestic violence organization or the courts. I would show her the research and tell to "RUN!!!!!!" Many mothers are fleeing out of America.

Domestic violence court lynched my life and as I sit here and write today, I am unemployed, receiving food stamps, and unable to work as a highly skilled and qualified E.R, ICU hospital nurse making $50-60/hr due to multiple fraudulent child support enforcements that went against my license and other oppressive and enslaving threats.

Judge Morgenstern being the overseer over this racketeering and corruption have snapped me and my children into poverty. My other 3 children have to pay for the fraud and crimes committed by this judge, "The Children Law Center, ACS, and the system of corruption ad practice of custody warmonger by this crime manipulating court. I have not spoken to my son now 6 years old. I will be arrested if I reach out to him because I have been speaking out about the crime-manipulation, and mother termination pattern of this court in New York city and other courts across the country. Her lawless orders are to humiliate me, smear me, and try to disempower me. She will never succeed. This is what a domestic violence judge did to me, and many others are doing while stealing, and embezzling money to any criminal that's willing to join in with them to keep the money flowing and the anti-family, and anti-mother agenda going.

"*God: My child is motherless, growing traumatically with a drug addicted-alcoholic-unfit, abusive dad, and this was in his best interest his lawyer, ACS, and the judge said.*"

Two weeks after my rigged custody case, another woman judge stole a baby and a toddler from their mom, a celebrity actress named Kelly Rutherford.

Kelly's custody ordeal cost her over 2 million dollars. A woman family court judge deported her children away from her and the legal processed bankrupted her.

"Dear God: why are judges botching and rigging custody cases, and snapping women and children into a life of rape, abuse, and poverty?"

Even though I know millions of stories of sexual abuse, and mothers having custody stolen away from them have been BLOCKED OUT

We are all familiar with the manipulation of Halle Berry to pay her assaulting-battering-ex-boyfriend child support.
PS due to crime manipulation GOOD fathers do not benefit from these court programs, only pedophiles-assaulters-and sociopaths that agree to harm women and children.

HALLE BERRY WANTS $16,000 CHILD SUPPORT PAYMENTS REDUCED; CLAIMS GABRIEL STOPPED WORKING AND IS LIVING OFF OF HER

I also notice the gatekeepers of these crimes were women, women judges, women lawyers, women ACS, CPS, evaluators enslaving and sacrificing children physically, sexually, and financially.

I am still in a learning process of all this mess. It feels like Satan hit me in the head with a bag of bricks.

I'm still trying to make sense of all of this. I have met women and other authors that 25 years touched on this topic and have made no progress, and seem like increasing of child enslavement and crime manipulation techniques that are rehearsed and practiced by the court ran AFCC and their ancillary companies.

So many evil women judges ripping children out of other women lives. Judges maternally depriving children of their mothers, this was eerily-evilly abnormal to me, especially researching numerous women judges were doing this to mothers. How the courts are mistreating mothers is straight out of the movie 'Changeling,' by Clint Eastwood

CHANGELING

ANGELINA JOLIE   JOHN MALKOVICH

A TRUE STORY

"Epic, taut, twisty and compelling."

The cover-up of the crimes in the courts are exactly like the
'FRANKLIN COVER-UP'

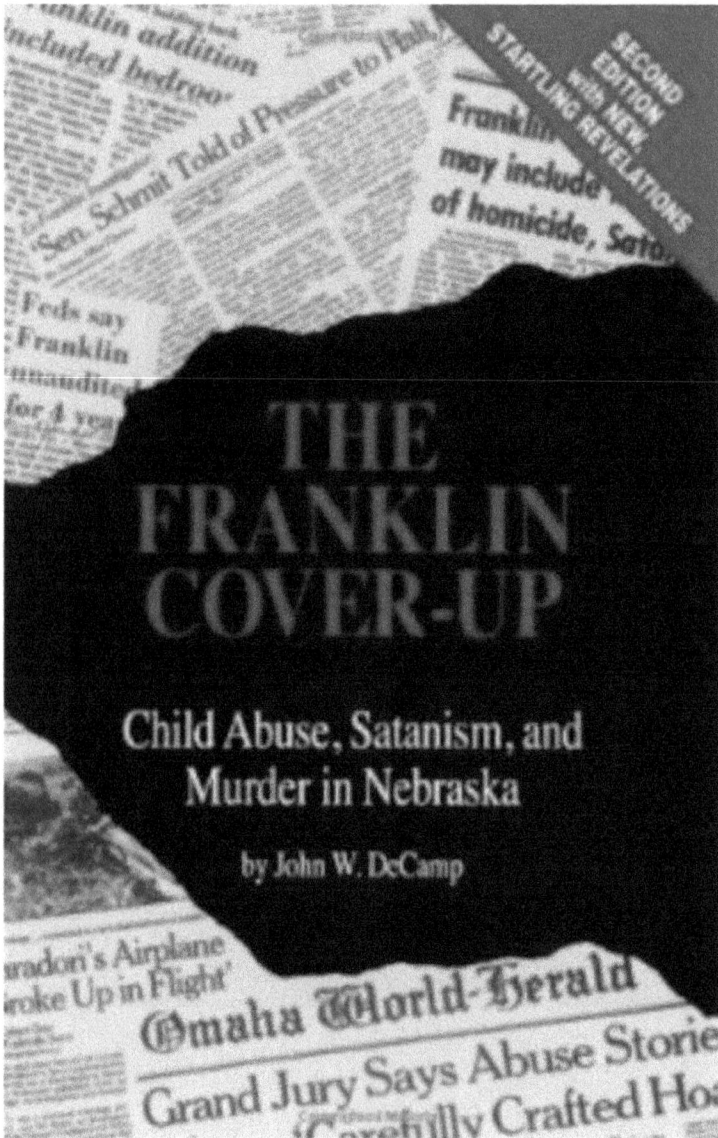

Thank you for purchasing this book. All money goes to helping moms and children in these ritual abusive courts.

If you would like to help make a difference contact us or donate
$3, $5, $10, whatever you can to stop crime manipulation against children, mothers, and women. When we stop crime we stop children having to be survivors. Email: HEALMothers@gmail.com

DONATE via PAYPAL to HEALMothers@gmail.com

Or send check or money order to:

Heal Network Inc.
P.O. Box 121070
Brooklyn, New York 11212

For More Information on Secret Court Crimes and Manipulation where Sex-offenders and Child-batterers, and harmers

are receiving having their crimes erased and gaining custody contact
HEAL Network's partner Organization

American Mothers Of Lost Children:
www.MothersOfLostChildren.org

American Mothers Of Lost Children:
www.MothersOfLostChildren.org

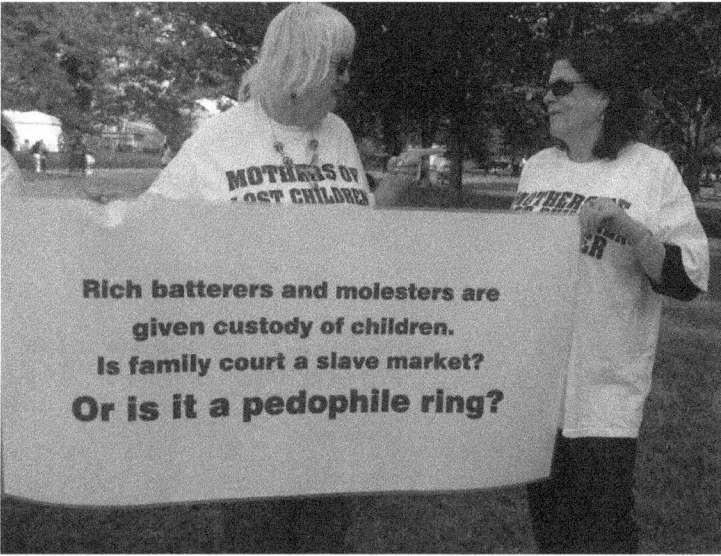

Guess who Benefits from Crime manipulation Tricks in these Courts? The 2% and others are bribed with tax-payer benefits.

Moms Protesting in front of the White House

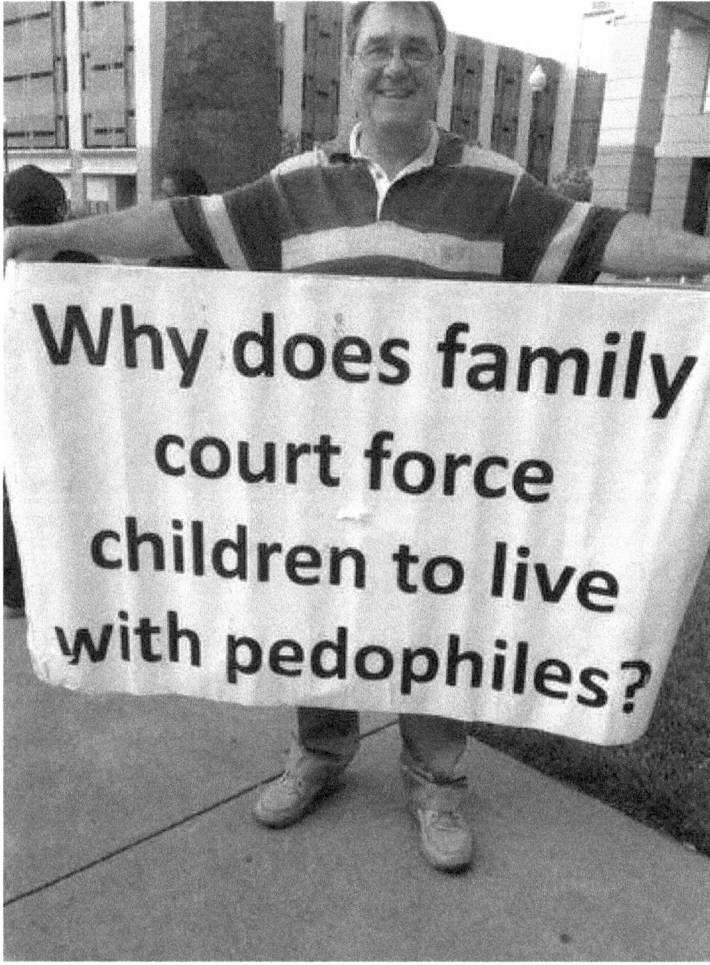

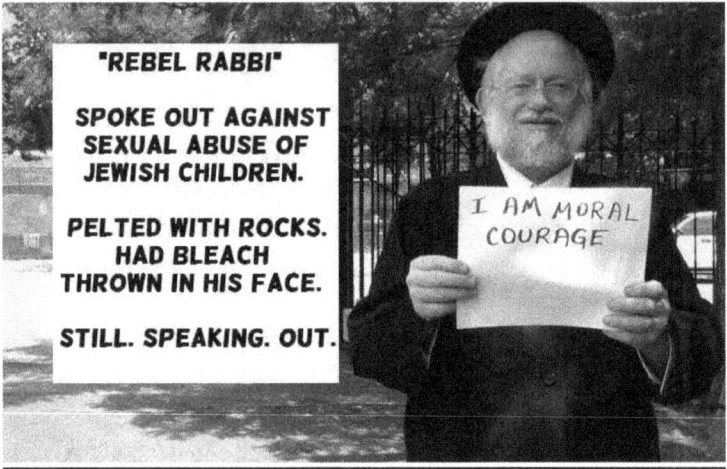

"REBEL RABBI"

SPOKE OUT AGAINST
SEXUAL ABUSE OF
JEWISH CHILDREN.

PELTED WITH ROCKS.
HAD BLEACH
THROWN IN HIS FACE.

STILL. SPEAKING. OUT.

I AM MORAL COURAGE

Rebel Rabbi with Vicki Polin fights against ritualistic sex abuse and violence to children. The Awareness Center, Inc., also known as the international Jewish Coalition against Sexual Abuse/Assault, is a nonprofit institution whose stated mission is to end sexual violence.
http://en.wikipedia.org/wiki/The_Awareness_Center

Amber Alert- Stop the system from lynching mothers and their children!

First Lawsuit for Child Abduction

- UNITED STATES DISTRICT COURT
EASTERN DISTRICT OF NEW YORK -
ALEAH HOLLAND R.N Individually and as
Founder of HEAL Network Inc.501c3,
ALEAH HOLLAND as mother/ Natural Guardian of
Howard Collins, a minor, as Mother and Natural Guardian of
ANNISSIA HOLLAND a minor,

-against-

Verified Complaint
Jury TRIAL Demanded

ESTHER M. MORGENSTERN, individually and in her capacity as
Justice of the Supreme Court of Kings County,

The CHILDREN's LAW CENTER;
GENEVIEVE TAHANG-BEHAN, ESQ in her individually and official
capacity, as a Lawyer of THE CHILDREN's LAW CENTER.
THE CITY OF NEW YORK;
NEW YORK CITY ADMINISTRATION FOR CHILDREN SERVICES,
RONALD E. RICHTER COMMISSIONER OF NEW YORK CITY
ADMINISTRATION FOR CHILDREN SERVICES, in his individual and
official capacity

PETER HARTLEY; ADMINISTRATION FOR CHILDREN SERVICES
SPECIAL ASSISTANT EXECUTIVE DEPUTY to COMMISSIONER in his
individual and official capacity,

NEW YORK CITY ADMINISTRATION FOR CHILDREN SERVICES CASEWORKERS, STACEY ROBINSON; in her individual and official capacity, MALIKA KHALSA ; in her individual and official capacity, SAMANTHA GRANT ; in her individual and official capacity,

NEW YORK CITY ADMINISTRATION FOR CHILDREN SERVICES SUPERVISORS INGRID WILLIAMS; in her individual and official capacity
Michael Chukwu in his individual and official capacity

CHRISTINE THEODORE,ESQ,
HOWARD COLLINS Sr.,
GRACIELA ALEXANDER a/k/a LADY LA LOCA,

Plaintiff ALEAH HOLLAND as Natural mother of Howard Collins jr., and Annissia Holland, both minors, ALEAH HOLLAND, collectively referred to herein as "Plaintiffs" complaining of the Defendants, respectfully allege all, upon belief as follows
PRELIMINARY STATEMENT

1. Plaintiffs bring this action for compensatory damages, punitive damages, and future attorneys' fees pursuant to 42 U.S.C. §1983 for the violation of their civil rights, as said rights are secured by said Statutes and the Constitutions of the State of new York and the United States Fourth and Fourteenth Amendment rights.

JURISDICTION

2. This action is brought pursuant to 42 U.S.C. §1983 and §1988 and the laws and the First, Fourth, Fifth, Sixth, Eighth and Fourteenth Amendments to the United States Constitution, by the Defendants employed by the City of new York, and Defendant under the color of the law in her capacity as a judge in the Superior Court of Kings County.

3. Jurisdiction is founded upon 28 U.S.C. §§ 1331, 1343(a)(3) and (4), 1367(a) and the doctrine of pendent jurisdiction.

VENUE

4.   Venue is properly laid in the Eastern District of New York under 28 U.S.C. §1391(b) in that this is the District in which substantial part of the events giving rise to the Plaintiffs' Claim.

5.   All Plaintiffs respectfully demand a trial by jury of all issues in this matter pursuant to the Seventh Amendment of the United States Constitution.

PARTIES

6. Plaintiffs Aleah Holland as the single mother of Howard Collins jr. (hereinafter referred to as Howard Jr., infant or Plaintiff), Infant Annissia Holland (hereinafter referred to as Annissia, infant, minor children, or Plaintiff), are and was at all times relevant to this Complaint a citizen and resident of the State of New York, citizens of the United States of America currently residing in Brooklyn, county of Kings.

7.   Plaintiff Aleah Holland is a stellar member of the community, a single mother, a Registered Nurse and the founder of HEAL Network, a 501c3 org that provides free afterschool services and basketball programs to children ages 5-20, HEAL Network Inc. provides free Saturday programs, free Health events to the community , and free services to Seniors living at home alone.

8.   Plaintiff Annissia Holland was born August 11, 1996. She is 15 years old when she was viciously and maliciously attacked by Defendant Howard Collins Sr. on June 27, 2012.

9.   Plaintiffs Howard Collins Jr. was born January 08, 2008. He was 4 years old on June 27th when he was viciously attacked by his father

Defendant Howard Collins while his sister Annissia Holland held him in her arms.

10. Defendant Esther Morgenstern is a justice Integrated Domestic Violence Court of the Kings County Supreme Court, Criminal Term in the 2nd Judicial District of New York presiding at 320 Jay Street, Brooklyn, New York. (Herein referred to as "Judge Morgenstern" or "Defendant" or 'IDV court") and took a Judiciary Oath of Office to enforce the laws of the State of New York.

11. Defendant City of New York (herein referred to as "NYC" or "Defendant") is a municipality that is a political subdivision of the State of New York.

12. Defendant New York City Administration for Children's Services, (hereinafter referred to as "ACS" or "Defendant") is a department working for NYC and or a subdivision and or department and or a branch of NYC.

13. Defendant, RONALD E. RICHTER at all times herein mentioned was the Commissioner of the New York City Administration for Children's Services.

14. Defendant, Peter Hartley at all times herein mentioned was New York City Administration for Children's Services Special Assistant to Executive Deputy Commissioner.

15. Defendant Stacey Robinson ACS caseworker at all times was employed by the New York City Administration for Children's Services.

16. Defendant Ingrid Williams is an ACS Supervisor to Stacey Robinson and at all times was employed by the New York City Administration for Children's Services.

17. Defendant Malika Khalsa ACS caseworker at all times was employed by the New York City Administration for Children's Services.

18. Defendant Michael Chukwu is an ACS Supervisor to Malika Khalsa, and at all times was employed by the New York City Administration for Children's Services.

19. Defendant Samantha Grant ACS caseworker at all times was employed by the New York City Administration for Children's Services

20. Christine Theodore, ESQ at all times was the 18-B attorney assigned to Howard Collins.

21. Genevieve Tahang-Behan, ESQ (hereinafter referred to as "Child law attorney§§§§§§§§", or "Defendant") at all times was employed by The CHILDREN's LAW CENTER and was Legal Guardian for Infant Howard Collins Jr.

22. Defendant HOWARD COLLINS Sr., natural father of Infant Howard Collins Jr.

23. Defendant GRACIELA ALEXANDER a/k/a LADY LA LOCA, natural paternal grandmother to Infant Howard Collins Jr.

24. The Administration for Children's Services, City of New York, instead of performing child protective services, as authorized under Article 10 of the Family Court Act, DEPRIVED PLAINTIFF AND PLAINTIFF's CHILDREN"S CIVIL RIGHT , 42 U.S.C section 1983; caused plaintiff and Plaintiffs' children, horrifying and grievous harm; deprived Plaintiffs' the right to family integrity; deprived plaintiffs' Constitutional rights.

25. Defendants, personally and through their agents, servants and/or employees, were acting under Oath of Office and color of the State Law and /or in compliance with the official rules, regulations, laws, statutes customs, usages and/or practices of the State of New York and/or the New York City Administration for Children's Services and/or The New York State Integrated Domestic Violence Court individually and together, conspired and acted in concert and did violate the constitutional rights of the Plaintiffs by retaliation, retribution, punishment, unusual and cruel decisions.

121

FACTUAL ALLEGATIONS

26. Plaintiffs' two children whom all suffered and some continue to be at risk of, severe abuse, maltreatment, neglect, and death.

27. Defendants, officials with responsibility for the Administration of Children Services, (ACS), which is an agency of the City of New York New York, intentionally mishandled plaintiffs' cases and deprived plaintiffs of their rights under the state and federal constitutions, as well as under numerous federal and state statutes. The child were severely neglected and abused, with knowledge of such abuse being made to the ACS, and the Court by mother Aleah Holland RN. Plaintiffs brought this action pursuant to 42 U.S.C. Section: 1983 seeking injunctive or declaratory relief and alleging violations of the Constitution, Child Welfare Act, Child Abuse Prevention and Treatment Act (CAPTA).

28. Accusations that all Defendants failed to respond to reports that the four-year-old boy was being beaten and abused, neglected, and maltreated, and life was and remains in danger.

29. August 15th, 2012 Acting under her Judiciary Oath of Office, Defendant Judge Esther Morgenstern, Supreme Court Justice RETALIATED, committing Malfeasance in office, unconstitutionally made ANOTHER Unusually Cruel decision to punish Plaintiffs Aleah Holland as well as her children.

30. August 15, 2012 Plaintiff Aleah Holland was notified by OWNER of Miracle Academy Daycare Keshon Puente, that Aleah Holland had a warrant out for her arrest by judge Morgenstern for not showing up to a court date, and that Judge Morgenstern had awarded custody of her son Howard Collins Jr.to father Howard Sr. Miracle Academy Daycare is the court ordered drop off and pick up location.

31. Howard Collins Sr. is known Drug Addict. Howard Collins on August 15th 2012 had an open criminal case for Assaulting a CHILD. Howard Collins on August 15th had an Order of Protection against him. Howard Collins notified Miracle Academy Daycare on June 11th he and his mom were getting cut off their welfare benefits and could

no longer provide for Plaintiff Howard Jr. , and that voucher for daycare would end August 24th, 2012

32. August 15th Aleah Holland received a letter in the mail by ACS worker Defendant Stacey Robinson stating "Aleah Holland had a warrant for her arrest issued by Judge Esther Morgenstern"

33. August 21st, 2012 Honorable judge Patricia Henry vacated the warrant against plaintiff Aleah Holland, and assigned her an attorney 18- B (Exhibit)

34. August 21, 2012 Plaintiff Aleah Holland asked for judge Morgenstern to be Recused from her case, to alleviate the abuse, maltreatment, neglect, domestic violence, and unusual and cruel punishment, on her and her children by all defendants.

35. Defendant Stacey Robinson from ACS was NOT to contact Aleah Holland ever again after July 20, 2012, for failing to protect infant Plaintiff Howard Collins Jr., and Annissia Holland

36. Stacey Robinson falsified documents from April19th to August 2012, lied, backdated documents, and stated there is no problem with illegal drug, illegal drugs use is okay (which I have her on recording)

37. Defendants all employees of ACS Stacey Robinson, Samantha Grant, and Malika Khalsa acting as agents of ACS has all falsified documents, downplayed abuse on Aleah Holland children, and acted in misconduct while employees of ACS, Plaintiff Aleah Holland reported all three.

38. Defendant Stacey Robinson screamed, yelled and ridiculed Plaintiff Aleah Holland for reporting abuse to her Commissioner on April 2018; in which Howard jr., stated he was burned with 'Weed" By Howard Sr. after returning from his 3rd weekend court ordered visit to Howard Senior's home.

39. Defendant Stacey Robinson corruption, intentionally failing to report what she saw in videos, intentionally failing to document

abuse by Howard Sr. failing to document on documents given to her by Plaintiff Aleah Holland, along with her bizarre mood swings, and erratic behavior had plaintiff Aleah Holland file numerous reports on her.

40. Even After reporting and filing complaints Defendant Stacey Robinson In May 2012 in July 2012 in August 2012 and September 2012 to ACS Commissioner, via 311 New York City Correspondences, and Peter Hartley directly through multiple emails; NOTHING was DONE.

41. Defendant Stacey Robinson continued to harass Plaintiff Aleah Holland, her daughter Plaintiff Annissia Holland, and live in fiancé Patrick Poux with unwanted unnecessary calls, and unannounced pop up visits at their home.

42. Defendant Stacey Robinson who Plaintiffs Aleah and Annissia Holland first met May 1 2012 failed to protect Howard Jr. from abuse, neglect, and maltreatment prior to June 27, 2012 and August 15th, 2012.

43. Defendant Stacey Robinson failed to do her job as an agent to ACS, instead she acted incompetent, malicious and jealous of Plaintiff Aleah Holland leading to endangering the lives of plaintiffs children Howard jr. and Annissia Holland would not have been attacked by Howard Collins on June 27th, 2012. She FAILED to put Safety Restrictions on Defendant Howard Collins Sr. and endangered the lives of Plaintiff children.

44. Defendants, judge Esther Morgenstern, ACS, The Child's lawyer, and Christine Theodore Co-conspired, in an overzealous effort to cover up the ongoing abuse, maltreatment, Domestic violence, and neglect of the Plaintiffs

45. Defendants made a conscious effort to intentionally LIE, to protect Howard Collins Sr. Defendant Judge Morgenstern made a conscious effort to hide Howard's Collins criminal charges of abusing a child, and order of Protection.

46. Defendants made a conscious malfeasance effort to harm Aleah Holland as a nurse, as a mother and as the Founder of HEAL Network Inc. a 501 C3 charity.

47. On July 18th, 2012 while Plaintiff Aleah Holland was at the hospital pregnant and bleeding, Defendant Judge Morgenstern without due process, while continuously denying Aleah Holland an attorney and without equal protection under the law, maliciously prosecuted plaintiff Aleah Holland which was unusual and cruel for a December 25th, 2010 incident in which Defendant Howard Collins Sr. was arrested for. Judge Morgenstern dismissed Howard Collins criminal charges for assaulting Aleah Holland on September 26, 2011 without probable cause.

48. On July 18th, 2012 Defendant Judge Morgenstern held a trial without Plaintiff Aleah Holland presence, and filed family criminal charges on Aleah Holland such as attempted assault, menacing, and harassment for the December 25th, 2010 incident Howard Collins Sr. was arrested for.

49. On July 18th 2012 defendant Judge Morgenstern dismissed plaintiff Aleah Holland PETITION of custody which Plaintiff attorney at the time Louis Floyd filed dated and stamped November 29, 2010 with PREJUDICE.

50. Judge Morgenstern reckless behavior and unusual and cruel orders caused extreme conflict between Plaintiff Aleah Holland and attorney Louisa Floyd who was appointed by Honorable judge Betty Stanton.

51. Defendant Judge Morgenstern made Plaintiff Aleah Holland feel attorney Louisa Floyd was incompetent. With her violating the law and abusing her power.

52. On August 15th, 2012 without Aleah Holland being notified to be present, Defendant Judge Morgenstern AWARDED defendant Howard Collins Sr. a known drug addict, and a known alcoholic CUSTODY of Howard Jr. Collins Sr.

53. August 15, 2012 for no safety or reasonable reason, not using common sense, Defendant Judge Esther Morgenstern denied custody and visitation rights to Plaintiff Aleah Holland, and removed youngest child Howard Collins Jr. making Plaintiff's child believe that his mom does not love him and has abandoned him.

54. Defendant Howard Collins, is unemployed was cut off of welfare benefits for FRAUD, was arrested for drugs and or violence in 2001, 2006, 2007, 2008, 2009, 2010, 2012.

55. Defendant Howard Collins Sr. Has, no High School diploma and no GED, or certified trade.

56. Defendant Howard Collins Sr. has a violent history and was shot in the foot before in relation to drug selling and gangs; which was not disclosed to Aleah Holland before entering into a relationship.

57. Howard Collins newest career is a gangster rapper, pimp, and an nonpaid alcoholic promoter of Angel Vodka

58. Defendant Howard Collins Sr. Was convicted in Atlanta , GA in 2000 for viciously stabbing someone, and pleaded guilty to drug sale in 2001. 2001 Howard Collins has a Domestic Violence charge for assaulting Tyra Frazier, Dante Frazier's mom.

59. Howard Collins Sr. a known, unemployed DRUG Abuser and alcoholic, as reported by the courts, test positive for illegal drugs EVERY day at the Bridge back to Life Rehab program since first being tested on Dec 12, 2011 was GRANTED custody of Howard Collins Jr. on August 15 2012 By Defendant Judge Morgenstern

60. Last time Plaintiff Howard Junior saw his father on June 27th, 2012 Howard Collins Sr. was viciously assaulting Howard Jr's sister Annissia Holland while she held Howard Jr in her arms.

61. Plaintiff Howard Jr stated his father burnt him with weed and punched him in the head in March 2012. I reported this to the courts, ACs, and Child lawyer, nothing was done.

62. Howard jr. stated numerous times to ACS workers that he did not want to live with Howard Collins Sr. or his grandmother lady la Loca.

63. Howard Collins jr. has always stated he wanted to live with his mother and sister each and every time he was asked by any ACS employee, child's lawyer, or anyone else.

64. Defendant Judge Morgenstern has violated Plaintiff Aleah Holland 1st, 4th, 5th, 6th, 8th, 14th Constitutional Rights. Abused her judicial power, and has acted above the LAW.

65. Defendant Judge Morgenstern and co-defendants denied custody of child Howard jr. to Plaintiff Aleah Holland the first time December 22, 2012 falsifying allegations identical allegations, of abuse, and guns that Aleah reported November 2010, in reference to Graciela alexander aka Lady La Loca pulling out guns and brandishing them on Howard Jr. and herself threatening a murder suicide.

66. Defendant Judge Morgenstern has treated litigant/ plaintiff Aleah Holland in a demonstrably egregious and hostile manner.
67. Defendant judge Morgenstern victimized Plaintiff Aleah Holland with her judicial corruption.

68. Defendant Judge Morgenstern has observed and conspired with attorneys Christine Theodore, Genevieve Tahang- Behan, and others reporting to her and investigating on her instructions to be untrustworthy, defaming, unethical, unlawful, deliberately indifferent, reckless, deceptive, malicious, unusually cruel, and extremely unprofessionally.

69. Defendant Judge Morgenstern and her codefendants have intentionally intimidated plaintiff and plaintiffs' children.

70. Defendant Judge Morgenstern in retaliation against Aleah Holland for reporting her to the Judicial committee numerous times, directed most investigative and executed actions knowingly utilizing false, and fabricated evidence resulting in fraudulent family offenses of attempted assault, menacing, and harassment.

71. May 09 2012 Defendant from The Children's Law Center stated on page. "I am glad his mom did put him in it. He says, his daddy smokes weed and uses needles.

72. Defendant Genevieve Tahang-Behan failed to protect Howard Collins Jr.

73. Defendant Genevieve Tahang-Behan attorney from the Children's Law Center- Howard Collins Jr law guardian, knew infant Howard's life was in and continues to remain in danger, knew he was being abused, neglected, maltreated, and had drug use and alcohol around him on a daily basis and did NOTHING to protect the child she was assigned to protect Plaintiff Howard Collins jr.

74. Defendant GENEVIEVE TAHANG-BEHAN was made aware that Howard Jr reported Howard Collins SR punched in him the head when he was mad. This was also reported to ACS. No action to protect Howard Jr. was ever taken ,and ACS documented, the abuse and maltreatment of child being punched in the head as "chastised the child"

75. Defendant Genevieve Tahang-Behan attorney from the Children's Law Center intentionally focused on a frivolous, false, fictitious, fabricated, defaming allegations for 6 months making false and misleading statements about Plaintiff Aleah Holland and her teen son plays with guns which defendant stated was a reported by (3)three year old child that defendant felt was extremely credible. Instead of the REAL ABUSE, and Misuse of Drugs that was going on in Howard Collins Sr. presence.

76. Defendant Genevieve Tahang-Behan attorney from the Children's Law Center continued for over 6 months with the false, frivolous, malicious, misleading accusations, and allegations, and intentionally refused to focus on facts such as her client Howard jr. life was endanger by being around a person that uses illegal drugs or buys illegal drugs on a daily basis, as well as use alcohol on a daily basis. She failed to focus on the danger her client was in.

77. When Plaintiff Aleah Holland reported the gun incident by Howard

Collins oldest son Dante Frazier from age of 10 years to 12 years old, and the adult neighbor Defendant Genevieve Tahang-Behan attorney from the Children's Law Center did NOTHING.

78. Defendant Genevieve Tahang-Behan attorney from the Children's Law Center intentionally failed to use common sense, and failed to acknowledge that mommy and my brother plays with guns, could have clearly been his brother Dante and his grandmother as reported numerous times.

79. When plaintiffs' attorney at the time Wynton Sharpe presented all parties with the recording on January 5th 2012, of Dante Frazier, Howard Collins Sr. oldest son talking about grandma Graciela Alexander aka Lady La Loca brandishing a gun in front of the children threatening to shoot herself and Howard Jr. the Defendants, Courts, and attorney to protect the child Genevieve Tahang-Behan did NOTHING.

80. Defendant Genevieve Tahang-Behan attorney from the Children's Law Center continued to be misleadingly, malicious, and with extreme bias, she continued to   repeat frivolous nonsensical issues to defame and attack plaintiff Holland and her older children, and not focus on the real dangers her infant client was in.

81. Defendant Genevieve Tahang-Behan attorney from the Children's Law Center being bias, and acting like a prosecutor, and investigator against Aleah Holland repeated hearsay that was reported to her by defendant Howard Collins Sr, which plaintiff Aleah Holland being less than 35 minutes late in over 2 years of picking up her son Howard jr. Defendant Behan on May 9th, 2012 stated misleading claims, false statements, and hearsay, defaming plaintiff Holland and her daughter Annissia Holland once again.

Genevieve Tahang-Behan: ("There was an issue where Miss Holland was late picking up my client. On that date the father and grandmother were called to stay with him until the mother arrived. When she did, her excuse was she was late because she had an incident with her daughter involving the police. I asked Mr. Collins to give me a release so I can speak to the children myself.)

82. Defendant Genevieve Tahang-Behan attorney from the Children's Law Center intentionally, wantonly, and maliciously focused for over 6 months on a frivolous claims, hearsay, and intentionally avoided facts of child she was designated to protect such as physical abuse, drug misuse and abuse, alcohol abuse, maltreatment to the child she was assigned to protect against Howard Collins senior.

83. Defendant Genevieve Tahang-Behan attorney from the Children's Law Center permitted the misuse of drugs by Howard Sr. in front of the child on a daily basis. She permitted the misuse of alcohol around her client Howard jr. on a daily basis.

84. Defendant Genevieve Tahang-Behan attorney from the Children's Law Center did nothing when defendant Howard Collins Sr. testing positive every day for drugs and alcohol went from DAILY testing to Random drug testing, even after her infant client stated he was beaten by dad, burnt by weed, and watched dad use weed and needles.

85. Defendant Genevieve Tahang-Behan attorney from the Children's Law Center allowed her infant client to witness drug abuse and use on a daily basis.

86. Defendant Genevieve Tahang-Behan attorney from the Children's Law Center misuses the law in various ways to slander, intimidate, defame, hurt, and abuse Plaintiffs and her children.

87. Defendant Genevieve Tahang-Behan attorney from the Children's Law Center allowed and continues to allows her client Howard Jr. life to be endangered physically, psychologically , and emotionally by a parent addicted to illegal drugs and alcohol.

88. Defendant Genevieve Tahang-Behan attorney from the Children's Law Center demonstrated gross negligence, incompetence and malpractice as an agent designated to PROTECT a child.

89. Defendant Judge Morgenstern allowed Plaintiffs children lives to be endangered by Howard Sr drug using, drug buying, and drug selling around the child she was assigned to protect.

90. After stating nonchalantly by child's lawyer Defendant GENEVIEVE TAHANG-BEHAN that father smokes weed and uses needles May 9 2012.

91. Defendant Judge Morgenstern AGAIN acted UNCONSTITUTIONALLY and denying Plaintiff Aleah Holland equal protection at the April 18 2012 and at May 9 2012 court date REFUSED Plaintiff Aleah Holland court appointed Legal Assistance with a totally different allegation less twenty one days of the 1st false reason.

92. Defendant Judge Morgenstern denied Plaintiff Aleah Holland legal representation on April 18th, 2012, from Aleah Holland tweet on Twitter about her manuscript on April 10th, 2012, lead plaintiff to know either Judge Morgenstern is one of the 800 followers on Twitter, or secretly discussing Plaintiff with the other side who may be secretly following her. Never since being in Judge Morgenstern court did plaintiff Aleah Holland ever say she made living writing books; which was Defendant Morgenstern reasoning for denying Aleah Holland legal representation, and equal protection on April 18th, 2012 and instead forced and intimidated Plaintiff Aleah Holland into representing herself against Plaintiff requests.

93. May 09th, 2012 Defendant Judge Morgenstern continuously denied Plaintiff Aleah Holland legal counsel and intimidated Plaintiff Aleah Holland to represent herself; and when Plaintiff Aleah Holland stated to the courts MY son is in DANGER! Nothing was done by anyone in legal power in the courts.

94. May 9th, 2012Defendant Judge Morgenstern went form DAILY drug TESTING to RANDOM DRUG TESTING.

95. June 27, 2012 both children were assaulted by Howard Collin Sr. who was arrested June 27th, 2012

96. Defendant Judge Morgenstern failed to protect Plaintiff and her children. She enabled and protected Howard Collins Sr. instead; after Howard Collins sr. tested positive EVERY DAY for illegal drugs and alcohol from December 2011 to May 9th, 2012, Judge Morgenstern

REDUCED his Drug Testing to RANDOM, and presently Howard Collins Sr has no drug or alcohol screening in place. She continued to REWARD Howard's abuse, and reckless behavior.

97. Defendant Judge Morgenstern while in her judicial oath of office and or judicial capacity along with codefendants, has intentionally abused, allowed abuse, assaults, violations, harm, and maltreated to all Plaintiffs.

98. Defendant Judge Morgenstern misuses the law in various ways to slander, intimidate, defame, hurt, and abuse Plaintiffs and her children.

99. Defendant Judge Morgenstern misuse Legal techniques, broke the rules, broke the laws, favored the other party, and allowed crimes to be committed against all Plaintiffs in her courtroom; due to the false and fabricated allegations, Plaintiff Aleah Holland has had her personal and professional reputation destroyed, being falsely and maliciously indicated as a person for child abuse and or neglect or maltreatment, as well as convictions of family offenses with a 2 year order of protection placed against her.

100.
Defendant Judge Morgenstern removed Howard Collins Jr. on August 15th, 2012 with no contact AT ALL by his mother Plaintiff Aleah Holland, who infant loves dearly. Plaintiff Aleah even begged for an emergency hearing on august 21st, 2012, went to at least 15 agencies for help to no avail, while Defendant judge Morgenstern went on Vacation, Howard Jr. mother continues until today of this complaint has No Contact at all with her son Howard Collins .

101.
Plaintiff Aleah Holland is suffering severely and praying to God that her son is okay every day as a result of Defendant Morgenstern unconstitutionally cruel baseless decision to punish her like this, not only take her son away but place him in a dangerous and drug addicted environment.

102.
Plaintiff Aleah Holland does not know how to explain where her

son Howard Jr. is, when asked at birthday parties, and family functions, and has to choose to avoid attending most family functions due to the humiliating and embarrassment, where family are used to seeing Howard Jr. at least 3 weekends out of the month.

103.
Plaintiff Howard Collins Jr. has suffered the loss of his primary caregiver and the loss of the close protective, safe, secure and loving relationship he needs, and has with his mother. Plaintiff Aleah Holland is mortified having her family and friends see her go through this Domestic Violence process for approximately 3 years and seen it result in these types of decisions, abuse, pain, personal relationships continue to suffer when reaching out for help.

104.
Defendant Judge Morgenstern is a threat to the public based on her biases, abuse of power, favoritism, unprofessionalism among other behaviors demonstrated such as professional misconduct, and retribution, as disregard for her judicial Oath of office, disregard for Plaintiffs civil, human, state, and Constitutional rights, and her unusual cruel punishments, as well as corruption demonstrated and allowed in her courtroom by unethical acting attorneys.

105.   The
actions of all the individual defendants, under their official oath of office, acting within the scope of their employment with the City of New York, deprived Plaintiffs of their rights under First, Fourth, Fifth, Eighth, and Fourteenth Amendments of the United States Constitution.

106.   The
negligent, unlawful, intentional, willful, deliberately indifferent, reckless intimidation and/or bad faiths acts and omissions of defendants caused Plaintiffs the following damage s, which continue to date and will continue into the future: personal injuries; pain; suffering; loss of liberty; severe psychological damage; infliction of physical injury and physical sickness, including but not limited to extreme stress, humiliation, indignities, and embarrassment; degradation, fear, loss of standing in the community; permanent loss

of natural psychological and social development; and restrictions on all forms of personal freedom including but not limited to diet, sleep, personal contact, educational opportunities, family vacations, travel, family relationships, enjoyment, and expression for which she is entitled monetary relief.

107.   Those same actions and omissions by defendants caused all plaintiffs to experience a loss of relationship with family at a crucial and tender age, including the financial support, nurture, love, guidance, and training that the mother Aleah Holland would have provided Howard jr. with during time loss,. This separation has led to severe emotional and psychological damage, infliction of physical injury and physical sickness, including but not limited to extreme stress, humiliation, embarrassment, and fear by Howard Jr leading him to believe his mother abandoned him and does not love him.

108.   The non-negligent acts and omissions committed by defendants described herein for which liability is claimed were done intentionally, unlawfully, maliciously, wantonly, recklessly, and or with bad faith, and said acts meet all of the standards for imposition of punitive damages, except as to claim against City of New York.

NATURE OF THIS ACTION

109.   This action seeks redress against the defendants for their unlawful, malfeasance, and egregious Conduct in violation of the Constitution of the United States and the rights there under, by falsely accusing plaintiff Aleah Holland of committing family offenses without her presence, removing her child on multiple occasions as retribution, dismissing Aleah Holland petition for custody with Prejudice, allowing tampering with children, domestic violence, abuse, maltreatment against her and her children; allowing mischaracterization, defamation, slander, misrepresentation, fabricating evidence, and making false statements , with a reckless disregard for the truth and blatantly omitting facts; and for conspiring to violate the human, civil, and constitutional rights of the plaintiff.

FEDERAL CLAIMS COUNT 1

42 .S.C § 1983 First, Fourth, Eighth, Fourteenth Amendment

110.

Plaintiffs hereby incorporate by reference all of the foregoing paragraphs 1 through 109 and further allege as follows:

111.

Defendants Judge Morgenstern, Christine Theodore, ESQ; Genevieve Tahang-Behan,ESQ; ACS, ACS caseworkers, supervisors NYC, Children's Law Center, failed to adequately investigate crimes drug use, domestic violence, and abuse by Howard Collins Sr, and Graciela Alexander and violated Plaintiffs clearly established rights of the United States Constitution to be free of unreasonable search and seizures, deprived of a family relationship absent compelling reasons, false family offenses, malicious prosecution to be based under the First, Fourth and Fourteenth Amendments

112.

Defendants Judge Esther Morgenstern, Christine Theodore, ESQ; Genevieve Tahang-Behan ESQ; ACS, ACS caseworkers, supervisors NYC, Children's Law Center, initiated and relentlessly continued prosecution of false, and fabricated claims in violation of Plaintiffs Aleah Holland clearly established constitutional rights.

113.

Additionally ,defendants Judge Morgenstern, Christine Theodore, ESQ; Genevieve Tahang-Behan ESQ; ACS, ACS caseworkers, supervisors NYC, Children's Law Center acting individually or in concert, ignored serious facts in front of them of drug use, child abuse, child maltreatment, child neglect, domestic violence, and Aleah Holland pleas of help for her and her children, thereby depriving her of her clearly established constitutional rights under the Fourth and Eighth, Fourteenth Amendment of the United States , including but not limited to her right to be free from Unusual and Cruel punishment, unreasonable searches and seizures.

114.

Defendants Judge Esther Morgenstern, Christine Theodore, ESQ;

Genevieve Tahang-Behan ESQ; NYC, Children's Law Center, ACS, ACS caseworkers, supervisors performed the described acts under color of state law, under oath of office, deliberately, intentionally, with malice or reckless disregard for the truth; in violation of their obvious basic duties to protect infants, and with deliberate indifference to infants 'clearly established constitutional rights.

115.   As a
direct and proximate result of defendants conduct, infant Howard Collins was removed from his mother, Plaintiff Aleah Holland, for a prolonged period and placed with a known unemployed drug abuser who burnt him, maltreated him and chastised him with punches to the head, as well had an order of protection against him for assaulting a child,, and an Open criminal Case, as other grievous and continuous damages and injuries set forth and above.

FEDERAL CLAIMS COUNT II
42.S.C § 1983 Fourteenth Amendment

116.
Plaintiffs hereby incorporate by reference all the foregoing paragraphs 1 through 115 and further allege as follows:

117.   The
defendants Judge Esther Morgenstern, Christine Theodore, ESQ; Genevieve Tahang-Behan ESQ; NYC, Children's Law Center, ACS, all of ACS caseworkers, supervisors ACS special assistant Peter Hartley, and commissioner RONALD E. RICHTER , acting in their official oath of office and acting in their conduct under color of state law had opportunities to intercede on behalf of Plaintiffs , to prevent mother Aleah Holland malicious prosecution, false family offenses, removal of maternal rights to one child Howard Collins jr., placed with known drug abuser with history of abuse against child stated as chastised, and deprivation of liberty without due process, and to prevent Plaintiffs from being separated, but, due to their intentional conduct and or reckless or deliberate indifference, declined or refused to do so.
118. The defendants Judge Esther Morgenstern, Christine Theodore, ESQ; Genevieve Tahang-Behan ESQ; NYC, Children's Law Center, ACS failures to intercede violated Plaintiffs clearly established

constitutional rights, included but not limited to not to be deprived of liberty without due process of law as guaranteed by the Fourth Amendment.

119. Defendants Judge Esther Morgenstern, Christine Theodore, ESQ; Genevieve Tahang-Behan ESQ; NYC, Children's Law Center, and ACS officers committed these acts under the color of state law, intentionally, with reckless disregard for the truth and with deliberate malicious indifference to Plaintiff as clearly established constitutional rights.

120. As a direct and proximate result of the defendants Judge Esther Morgenstern, Christine Theodore, Children's Law Center officer ESQ; NYC, ACS officers' actions Aleah Holland was wrongly prosecuted, denied access to her child Howard Collins Jr. was placed with a known unemployed drug abuser, with an current criminal case for assaulting a child, and Plaintiff suffers and continues to suffer other grievous and continuing damages and injuries set forth above.

FEDERAL CLAIMS COUNT III
42.S.C § 1983 First, and Fourteenth Amendment

121. Plaintiffs hereby incorporate by reference all the foregoing paragraphs 1 through 120 and further allege as follows:

122. During time infant Howard Collins was detained and removed from custody of Aleah Holland, Plaintiffs suffered the loss they had of a loving safe relationship, as well as the mortification of having her child taken away from her and placed with a known drug abuser.

123. At the same time Plaintiffs suffered separation, anxiety, and Plaintiff Aleah Holland suffered the terrible knowledge that her child Howard jr. is continuing to experience harm as foresaid. To the extent that custodial plaintiffs can establish that the conditions of placing child with a Known Drug Abuser, who is unemployed, and with a current criminal case for assaulting a child, and allegations of abusing child recently, is so inadequate as it violate plaintiffs' Fourteenth Amendment due process right to be free from harm, which they are entitled to do so.

124. Defendants Judge Esther Morgenstern, Christine Theodore, ESQ; Genevieve Tahang-Behan ESQ; NYC, Children's Law Center, and ACS officers acting individually and in concert, by their conduct, including refusing to remove child from Howard Collins Sr, a known drug abuser, with numerous accusations of abusing , maltreating, and or neglecting infant Howard and placing him with custody of the child with no contact by his Mother Plaintiff Aleah Holland, deprived plaintiffs of their clearly established constitutional rights under the First, and Fourteenth Amendments of the United States Constitution, including but not limited to the rights to family association, for a parent to live with their child, and to participate in their infants education, nurturing, development, care, protection and safety for their infants, and infants right to the love, care, protection, guidance, support, security, and nurturing of their parents.

125. Defendants Judge Esther Morgenstern, Christine Theodore, ESQ; Genevieve Tahang-Behan ESQ; NYC, Children's Law Center, and ACS officers committed these acts under color of state law, intentionally, maliciously, highly outrageously, with reckless disregard and/or deliberate indifference to plaintiffs safety as well as close relationship and clearly established constitutional rights, and with full knowledge that their actions would interfere with the relationship between Plaintiffs.

126. As a direct and proximate result of defendants Judge Esther Morgenstern, Christine Theodore, ESQ; Genevieve Tahang-Behan ESQ; NYC, Children's Law Center, and ACS officers' Plaintiff Aleah Holland was maliciously prosecuted, had false family offenses placed on her, had her child removed from her home and her life during which infant safety, rearing, and nurturing suffered because of infant Plaintiff's absence, as well as other grievous and continuing damages and injuries set forth.

STATE LAW CLAIMS
COUNT IV
Malicious Prosecution and False Conviction

127. Plaintiffs hereby incorporate by reference all the foregoing paragraphs 1 through 126 and further allege as follows:

128. Defendants Judge Esther Morgenstern with malice, malfeasance and or gross negligence, acting individually or in concert filed fraudulent charges on Aleah Holland which is in place for 2 years. At the trial without legal representation, and Aleah Holland presence Judge Morgenstern found Plaintiff Aleah Holland guilty of Harassment, Menacing, and attempted assault without the right of due process.

129. Defendants Judge Esther Morgenstern with malice, malfeasance and or gross negligence, acting individually or in concert charged and convicted Plaintiff Aleah Holland for crimes Howard Collins Sr was arrested for on December 25, 2010, in violation of the laws of New York.

130. Defendants Judge Esther Morgenstern engaged in these acts within her judiciary scope of her employment, and are entitled to indemnification.

131. As a direct result and proximate result of defendant judge Morgenstern conduct Aleah Holland was maliciously prosecuted, denied legal representation, denied due process, falsely convicted of harassment, menacing, and attempted assault, had her infant child taken away from her and suffers the other grievous and continuing damages and injuries set forth and above.

COUNT V
Intentional, Reckless, Malfeasance, Malicious Abuse of Process, and Infliction of Emotional Distress

132. Plaintiffs hereby incorporate by reference all the foregoing paragraphs 1 through 131 and further allege as follows:

133. The improper, deliberate, and traumatizing conduct of all defendants Judge Esther Morgenstern, Christine Theodore, ESQ; Genevieve Tahang-Behan ESQ; NYC, Children's Law Center, and ACS officers, in failing to protect Plaintiffs Aleah Holland and her children, refusing to truthfully investigate, refusing to investigate readily verifiable claims resulting in wrongful, unlawful removal of one child placing him with a known child abuser, with a current criminal case for assaulting a child leading to severe emotional distress, is extreme, and outrageous. It directly and proximately caused Plaintiffs to suffer the grievous and continuing injuries, and damages set forth above.

134. In the alternative, all defendants negligently, and grossly negligently, and in breach of their duties owed to Infants and Plaintiffs' report truthfully, accurately the information given to them; report factually the information taken from witnesses, and their investigative responses to such information; and investigate readily verifiable claims of child being in danger due to drug abuse, drug use around infants, as well as physical, emotional, psychological abuse, as well as domestic violence which caused plaintiff Aleah Holland to be maliciously prosecuted in bad faith, and had her youngest child removed from her, Defendants actions unreasonably endangered infant physical health, and safety, and caused infants to suffer physical harm, including physical ailments resulting from the circumstances and duration of infant Howard Collins being neglected, maltreated, and abused, and wrongful removal, and infant Annissia Holland being assaulted, emotionally , and psychologically abused. Defendants further inflicted emotional distress on Plaintiffs by unlawfully depriving them of the relationship, with all previously identified injuries' attendant thereto.

135. All of the aforementioned acts 1 through 135 deprived the Plaintiffs of the right, privileges, and immunities guaranteed to citizens of the United States by the First, Fourth, Fifth, Eighth, and fourteenth Amendments of the United states of America and in violation of 42 U.S.C. § 1983

136. As a result of the foregoing, Plaintiff Aleah Holland was deprived of her liberty, were denied fundamental constitutional rights, was denied due process, was denied equal protection under the law, was publicly embarrassed and humiliated, was caused to suffer severe

emotional distress, was caused exclusion from a career as a nurse, and working in her capacity as the Founder of HEAL Network Inc. a 501 c3 organization and had her personal and professional reputation destroyed.

137.Defendants Judge Esther Morgenstern, Christine Theodore, ESQ; Genevieve Tahang-Behan ESQ; NYC, Children's Law Center, and ACS officers engaged in these acts within the scope of their employment and are entitled to indemnification pursuant to Gen. Mun. Law §§ 50-j, 50k and 50-1 and by contract.

COUNT VI
Negligence

136. Plaintiffs hereby incorporate by reference all foregoing paragraphs 1 through
135 and further alleges as follows:

137. All defendants Judge Esther Morgenstern, Christine Theodore, ESQ; Genevieve Tahang-Behan ESQ; NYC, Children's Law Center, and ACS officers are liable for negligence, having breached their duty of reasonable care and protection of infants.

138. Specifically, without limitation and by way of example, defendants:

a.   Despite their notice and knowledge, as outlined above, failed to investigate Aleah Holland claims of domestic violence, drug misuse, abuse, maltreatment, and neglect;

b.   Despite their notice and knowledge, failed to adequately protect plaintiffs from physical and emotional injury despite having a reasonable amount of time and opportunity to do;

141

c. Despite their notice and knowledge failed to protect plaintiffs' constitutional rights.

d. Despite their notice and knowledge deprived plaintiff of federal civil rights

e. Despite their notice and knowledge as outline above used illegal process to convict Plaintiff Aleah Holland of family offenses

f. Despite their notice and knowledge defendants acted with intent to do harm to the plaintiffs without excuse of justification

139. Defendants negligence and gross negligence directly and proximately caused Plaintiffs to be assaulted, abused, and maltreated, caused plaintiff Aleah Holland to be maliciously prosecuted, falsely convicted, defamed, slandered, and had her youngest child wrongly taken away from her with no contact at all unless she would be arrested.

COUNT VII
Respondeat Superior Claim against City of New York

140. Plaintiffs hereby incorporate by reference all of the foregoing paragraphs 1 through
139 and further allege as follow:

141. At all times relevant to this complaint, the individual defendants, and or defendants
Judge Esther Morgenstern, Christine Theodore, ESQ; Genevieve Tahang-Behan ESQ;
NYC, Children's Law Center, and ACS officers acted as agents of the City of New York, or allowed by the city of New York to do business in the City of New York including law enforcement functions, of those entities, and within the scope of their employment or agency with those entities

142. The conduct by which the defendant officers, prosecutors, and judge committed the torts of malicious prosecution, intentional, reckless, with bad faith, or negligent infliction of distress, and negligence, was not undertaken for the individual defendants

personal motives, but rather was undertaken while the individual defendants were on duty, carrying out routine investigative functions, as judges, child law prosecutors, and engaging in such conduct as would have been reasonably expected by their employers. Indeed, the conduct of the individual defendants in committing the above-described torts was reasonably and foreseeable by the City of New York.

143. The Plaintiff was prosecuted to an unconstitutional selected enforcement of the penal law in violation of the Equal Protection clause of the Constitution of the United States.

144. The Defendants' motive for prosecuting the Plaintiff Aleah Holland, and not prosecuting the person arrested, and who actually committed the acts of violence, abuse, and maltreatment against Plaintiffs', and continued after being arrested continued to assault, abuse, maltreat, and neglect Plaintiffs, were not based on any rational basis.

145. Under the doctrine of respondeat superior, the City of new York are liable for their agents' state law torts of malicious prosecution, intentional, reckless, or negligent infliction of emotional distress, and negligence.

WHEREFORE, Plaintiffs prays for the following relief:

a.   Damages, in an amount to be established at trial , as compensation for injuries to reputation, emotional suffering, past, and future economic losses, invasion of privacy, constitutional deprivations, loss of professional opportunities, loss of future career prospects, legal and other expenses, and other injuries proximately caused and enhanced by defendants', wrongful conduct; jointly against ALL defendants in the amount of $999,999,999,999,999.99 .

b.   Damages, in an amount to be established at trial, to punish defendants for fraudulent, willful reckless, wanton, and malicious conduct; to punish defendants for outrageous conduct pursued with actual malice that recklessly and callously disregarded plaintiffs' physical and emotional well-being and constitutional rights; to discourage defendants from engaging in similar conduct in the future; and to deter others similarly situated from engaging in similar wrongful conduct; all defendants in the amount of $999,999,999,999,999.00

c. That the court award punitive damages to plaintiffs', and against all individual defendants, in the amount to be determined at trial by jury.

d. Judge Morgenstern be disbarred
e. For trial by jury
f. An award of attorneys' fees and customary cost, expenses, and interest incurred in pursuit of this action; and
g. Any relief deemed just and proper Plaintiffs may be entitled too

Dated September 27, 2012

A Little Lynched/ Amber Alert

www.ingramcontent.com/pod-product-compliance
Lightning Source LLC
Chambersburg PA
CBHW032002040426
42448CB00006B/463